A Note on the Readings

This guide follows the Sunday Lectionary for Year B. The gospel is always given, and occasionally other readings are included as well. The readings have not been modified or paraphrased, but in some instances they have been abridged. The citation given in this book is always to the full text of the reading as given in the Lectionary.

YEAR B

PREACHING & TEACHING the GOSPELS to CHILDREN

SEAN McENTEE

THE COLUMBA PRESS
TWENTY-THIRD PUBLICATIONS

The Scripture used in this volume is from the *New Revised Standard Version* (with Apocrypha). Copyright 1989, A Division of Christian Education of the National Council of the Churches of Christ in the United States of America. Published by Oxford University Press, New York.

Published simultaneously in Ireland by
The Columba Press
93 The Rise
Mount Merrion, Blackrock
Co. Dublin
ISBN 1-85607-086-7

Twenty-Third Publications
185 Willow Street
P.O. Box 180
Mystic CT 06355
(203) 536-2611
800-321-0411

ISBN 0-89622-569-0
Library of Congress Catalog Card Number 93-60368

CONTENTS

INTRODUCTION 1

THE SEASON OF ADVENT

First Sunday of Advent 5
Second Sunday of Advent 8
Third Sunday of Advent 11
Fourth Sunday of Advent 14

THE SEASON OF CHRISTMAS

Christmas 17
Holy Family 20
Second Sunday After Christmas 24
Epiphany 26
Baptism of the Lord 28

THE SEASON OF LENT

First Sunday of Lent 30
Second Sunday of Lent 33
Third Sunday of Lent 36
Fourth Sunday of Lent 39
Fifth Sunday of Lent 43
Passion Sunday 45

EASTER

Easter Sunday 48

THE SEASON OF EASTER

Second Sunday of Easter   50
Third Sunday of Easter   53
Fourth Sunday of Easter   56
Fifth Sunday of Easter   59
Sixth Sunday of Easter   62
Ascension   64
Seventh Sunday of Easter   67
Pentecost Sunday   70

FEASTS OF THE LORD IN ORDINARY TIME

Trinity Sunday   73
The Body and Blood of Christ   76

SUNDAYS IN ORDINARY TIME

Sundays in Ordinary Time   79

INTRODUCTION

Whether we are planning homilies for children or teaching about the Sunday gospels in the classroom, we have to think like teachers. Teachers think very purposefully. A lesson in the classroom has a beginning, a middle, and an end, dictated by insights from psychology, sociology, and education.

A teacher's lesson plan is guided, first of all, by an overall learning objective. A theme or topic to be learned goes through the steps of:

(a) being introduced,

(b) being explored and enlarged, and

(c) being reinforced through learning activities.

These steps come from a larger learning theory that proposes principles that preachers have to bear in mind.

Children think concretely.

Children learn out of their own range of limited life experiences.

Children work out of a strong sense of feeling (which is supported as they grow older by an equally strong intellectual activity).

Children learn through activity (a teacher provides appropriate learning opportunities and activities for children).

I have followed a teaching style and process in preparing this book for preachers. Although the material presented here is focused on the homilist, teachers should find it equally useful for introducing the gospels in the classroom. Here are the steps I follow for each Sunday:

Overview

Step One	Focusing Experiences
Step Two	Exploring the Word of God
Step Three	Call to Faith
Step Four	Call to Action

Overview

In the Overview for each Sunday, the key issues of the gospel are outlined and clarified, perhaps, by adding some biblical or liturgical background. From this adult perspective the preacher is encouraged to move down a gear into the cultural, emotional, linguistic, and experiential world of children to accommodate children's insights, experiences, and ways of learning. The challenge presented to children will then be seen to have devolved from a larger picture and not be in any way arbitrary, artificial, or free-floating.

The Overview is the device we use for alerting preachers and teachers to the overall thrust of the gospel; it also suggests an approach that seems to meet the needs of children.

Step One: Focusing Experiences

By focusing on appropriate experiences from the child's world we are creating emotional and experiential access routes for the gospel message. We are creating a friendly environment, a friendly atmosphere for the gospel. We are creating a receptivity in the child's mind, a row of antennae that are tuned in to what the gospel will be saying.

These are called focusing experiences because they focus the child's attention, interest, and feeling on the issues that the gospel will address.

Step Two: Exploring the Word of God

Here we explore and enlarge. The gospel story is the vital element. We cannot presume that the story has been heard in the course of the formal reading. We have to tell it again, this time adding our own style, our own nuances, our own phrases, our enlargements of character, our refinements of feelings, our local coloring. Now each one of us is storyteller to the children. The gospel proclaimed a few moments previously needs more work, needs to be enlarged a little, needs to be spoken differently, needs to be delivered differently. The gospel needs to be supported by words children use, by gestures and inflections children understand.

The gospel story is full of richness, color, and power. We have to dance and weave a little with the story. We need to warm to the story, get into it, and make it our own. Our own personal echoes and style have to reverberate through the story. We are all storytellers at heart. Given the right audience we delight in telling stories. This is our opportunity to tantalize!

We should not sideline the gospel story to deliver moral or doctrinal points. The story should not be disposed of in a few summary sentences. This tendency to use the gospel story as a quarry for points came from the days when preachers felt the need to give points of doctrine a constant airing. An apologetical approach had precedence over a scriptural approach. The story was not given a chance to interact with the imagination. The gospel stories do not tire easily but they must be told in a way that stokes the imagination. And children are all feeling and imagination!

Stories work their own magic, have a life of their own, leave their own traces. The biblical stories and anecdotes continue to rattle around inside us and reappear at odd moments. The wonderful thing about a story is that it grows with us. It challenges us as we are, at whatever level of experience we're at.

We must not avoid gospel stories about death, hell, sheep and goats, damnation and the gnashing of teeth. These judgment stories are not news items or mathematical details or historical descriptions to frighten the children; they are stories to inhabit their imagination, to help their reflection, to help their search for wisdom. They will find a way to accommodate a God of love with a God of judgment.

In this book the gospel story forms the heart of the homily. Many of the stories are retold in a familiar way to hint at a style the homilist might follow.

We may decide to use a questions technique in a dialogue homily situation, to interact with the listening/learning group. It is suggested that questions should follow a pattern, starting first with factual questions, then following with feeling and insight questions.

Step Three: Call to Faith

We need to enunciate, as simply and directly as possible, the call of the readings. In this book, the call is a simple speech linked to the focusing, telling, and exploring that went before. It is a natural high point in which the threads are all pulled together. It is a moment of vision, challenge, and appeal. In this moment we make the Word of God active for the children.

Step Four: Call to Action

The Call to Action clarifies and underlines the Call to Faith. We organize actions that reinforce the call and challenge of this gospel. The actions suggested must be practical and possible for children. The purpose of these actions is to suggest the intimate connection between liturgy and life, between hearing the Word and doing the Word. It is an important part of the whole process. As teachers always say, doing is vital to learning! I have suggested some actions that seemed to have worked well. You will, of course, need to adapt and supplement these to suit your own particular circumstances.

Integrating the Homily

Those who used *Preaching and Teaching the Gospels to Children (Year A)*, last year, will have noticed that

(a) the homily was concentrated on those moments immediately after the reading of the gospel;

(b) the homily depended largely on a word approach—concentrated on words, ideas, and images.

This seemed to work and the feedback has been excellent, but I thought we should try some new strategies for this year (Year B). So, in this volume the strategy for delivering the homily is more integrated:

(a) The homilist works harder to highlight the gospel story as a story with its own twists and turns.

(b) The homily is seen to have links with the whole Mass, links with the penitential service at the beginning right through to links with the solemn blessing at the end of Mass.

(c) More emphasis is put on action elements as part of the homily—prayers, songs, litanies, processions, testimonies from people in the community.

(d) the Call to Faith and the Call to Action are integrated as part of the delivery of the homily.

(e) As per last year, action elements for home or school are linked to the thoughts arising in the homily and are suggested as follow-up possibilities.

A Last Word

Preachers sometimes do not start at the beginning. In this book the steps of the learning process are interchangeable. We may start, on occasions, not with the Focusing Experiences but with the Call to Action and follow with the Exploration of the Word. We are at liberty to work either backward or forward through the steps. The hearing of the Word of God is enriched for the children by a variety of approaches.

First Sunday of Advent

Gospel
A reading from the holy Gospel according to Mark (13:33–37)

Jesus said, "Beware, keep alert; for you do not know when the time will come. It is like a man going on a journey, when he leaves home and puts his slaves in charge, each with his work, and commands the doorkeeper to be on the watch. Therefore, keep awake—for you do not know when the master of the house will come, in the evening, or at midnight, or at cockcrow, or at dawn, or else he may find you asleep when he comes suddenly. And what I say to you I say to all: Keep awake."

The gospel of the Lord.

Overview
Mark puts us on notice to be on round-the-clock lookout for that great day and those new times—the *parousia*—when the Lord Jesus will come in glory. The story is meant to inspire and warn. Those who keep a good lookout are rewarded; those who are lackluster are excluded from the good times with God.

For the children, we should focus on preparation for Christmas through the wider theme of being on the alert to protect the things of God.

Focusing Experiences
Parents and teachers should help the children understand that Advent is a season of preparation for Christmas. We have to get in shape for welcoming Jesus. We have to get in the mood. We have to let the thought of Jesus and what he means sink into our hearts. This can be done by creating an Advent mood at home or in school by preparing an Advent wreath and also through prayer, talk, exercises, songs, pictures, and posters. The liturgy of each Sunday of Advent will also get us thinking about Christmas.

On the first Sunday of Advent we are invited to guard the things of God in our lives. Jesus spent his life reminding people of God's love. God's love is too precious to have it snatched away from us or lost through neglect.

The focusing experiences for this Sunday might include a discussion on security. Jesus talked about security in his day and this led him to talk about putting security on the things of God in our lives.

Children of this generation have a heightened sense of the security business and an awareness of the most sophisticated electronic surveillance systems. Ask the children if they have security systems on their house. Is it well protected from robbers?

Draw up a plan from the best of what they've seen on TV:
security lights
video cameras
electronic buzzers in every room
infrared heat detectors
pressure plates
doors that open to a secret code
a doorkeeper
passwords
guard dogs
alarms
security guards
watchman

Exploring the Word of God

In the days of Jesus people also talked about security. In those days everyone agreed that the best security you could have on your house was a doorkeeper. The doorkeeper watched everybody and everything, saw people in and out of the house, and did night duty, too. The doorkeeper didn't fall asleep. He never, ever left the door unguarded. He was always on guard, keeping an eye out, wide awake.

People who had good doorkeepers considered themselves very lucky indeed. Doorkeepers who kept a sharp eye on the comings and the goings around the owner's house were highly regarded. The wealthy owners couldn't be without them. Jesus praised the good doorkeepers who knew how to stay on the watch and be on their guard.

Call to Faith

Jesus said we all had to become doorkeepers, defenders, guardians, security people. Why? To guard and defend the things of God in our lives. Jesus said we had to watch out for the things of God, and to stay away from the people and things that put our friendship with God at risk. God's Spirit lives in us. We have to protect and defend that Spirit. If our security is lax we will lose the Spirit. The Spirit can only be present where there is peace and love and harmony. If we let disharmony or violence or other evils breach our security we will be big losers of the things that count with God.

Get your security right! Guard the things of God in your lives. Be on the watch. Don't be slack or casual. What you have from God is worth defending. Defend it.

Call to Action

During the Mass repeat the challenge and the slogan to be alert to the things of God—at the prayer of the faithful and in a reflection after communion. Pay special attention to the eucharistic prayer. Help the children to be alert to the things of God in it.

Help the children think of Christian organizations they might join to help them become more alert to the things of God.

Begin developing programs of prayers or deeds at home to remind the children of Jesus and what he stands for.

Help them organize their families to listen to an occasional session of songs that have Christian themes.

Second Sunday of Advent

Gospel
A reading from the holy Gospel according to Mark (1:4–8)

John the Baptizer appeared in the wilderness, proclaiming a baptism of repentance for the forgiveness of sins. And people from the whole Judean countryside and all the people of Jerusalem were going out to him, and were baptized by him in the river Jordan, confessing their sins. Now John was clothed with camel's hair, with a leather belt around his waist, and he ate locusts and wild honey. He proclaimed, "The one who is more powerful than I is coming after me; I am not worthy to stoop down and untie the thong of his sandals. I have baptized you with water; but he will baptize you with the Holy Spirit."

The gospel of the Lord.

Overview
John the Baptist has a colorful personality. He is wild and primitive and exciting! Children like personalities. John is odd in an attractive way. He's the stuff of which gurus, musical people, and pop stars are made.

Apart from being unusual (like Elijah in the Bible), John has a serious agenda to put across. He is a totally committed advance publicity man for Jesus. He has a passion for the job. He is driven by the Spirit. We introduce John to the children both as a personality and as someone bursting with a keenness to tell his news about Jesus.

The liturgical setting of this second Sunday of Advent asks for continued preparation for Christmas.

Focusing Experiences
There must be a local colorful character, or someone on television or from history, who reminds parents of John the Baptist, someone with John-the-Baptist qualities—dedication to a cause, eccentric, carefree, single-minded, committed. Parents and teachers can share their observations with the children. Then there is John's advance publicity campaign announcing Jesus. We are also familiar with publicity campaigns. Share your insights with the children.

Exploring the Word of God

It's John the Baptist. Listen to him: "Change your ways! Stop sinning! Come back to the paths of God! Turn back to God who loves you! Walk once again with God. God will forgive you. Make a straight path for the Lord who comes among you."

People went out into the wilderness to hear him. That's where he lived—out there under the sun and the stars, alone with the animals and with God. People came out of the city of Jerusalem, out of houses and apartments searching for him because they heard that God was in him like in none other. They walked miles and miles to get a sight of him. They went out to him in droves. People came from Judea, too—country people who were seeking God in this great man.

He was a holy man, a saint. Everybody sensed that. They wanted to hear him, hear his words, be near him, see him with their own eyes, feel the goodness flowing from him, be in his presence, touch him, confess their sins to him, make a promise to him to change their ways and walk with God once more.

He had charisma. He had a way about him. Once they met him people loved him. They followed him with their eyes and hung on his words. They wanted to stay with him. They wanted to change their ways because he asked them to.

His name was John the Baptist.

He wore strange clothes, things he had picked up in the wilderness: a long shirt made from camel's hair, a leather belt, leather sandals.

He looked different—different from people who lived in towns and villages. John actually looked like a prophet. There was a passion in his eyes, a fire, a determination, a conviction, a belief, and a gentleness. He was a man of God.

And he persuaded people to change their ways. His voice was magic. It was easy to go along with him. What he said made sense. And those who wanted to turn back to God walked with him into the river Jordan to be baptized into a new way with God.

But then he took the spotlight off himself. He spoke of someone great and wonderful who was to come. And to all the eager people gathered around he made a declaration. "The man who will come after me is much greater than I am. I am not good enough to bend down and untie his sandals." It was a shock to hear such humble words from so great a man, so wonderful a prophet.

The people wondered who was the one destined to come among them. Who was this person that John spoke about with such great respect? Who was this person who would change the world? They knew from the way John made his announcement that the person he was proclaiming was at least a mighty prophet. A new prophet from God? Who knows? Maybe even the Messiah who would lead people into new times and a new way of living. And there was a buzz of excitement over the whole country round about.

Call to Faith

We are called to meet John. We are called to hear John's good news. We are called to welcome the new times of which he speaks. We are called to change our ways, to get in tune with the new times and the new days. We are called to renew our friendship with Jesus.

Call to Action

Sing or listen to a hymn or ballad about John the Baptist.

Have someone do a John the Baptist speech—fiery and colorful, a call to renewal—as a way of welcoming Jesus. (There must be a young actor/actress in the parish who would be willing to give it a try. If this is done at Mass, use it as a post-communion reflection.)

Consider organizing a one-day retreat of renewal in preparation for Christmas, with songs and drama, discussion, videos, and activities.

Prepare a plan of action for a publicity campaign to promote the name of Jesus, God's own voice among the people. Prepare handouts for your imagined door-to-door campaign.

THIRD SUNDAY OF ADVENT

Gospel
A reading from the holy Gospel according to John (1:6–8,19–28)

This is the testimony given by John when the Jews sent priests and Levites from Jerusalem to ask him, "Who are you?" He confessed and did not deny it, but confessed, "I am not the Messiah." And they asked him, "What then? Are you Elijah?" He said, "I am not." "Are you the prophet?" He answered, "No." Then they said to him, "Who are you? Let us have an answer for those who sent us. What do you say about yourself?" He said,

"I am the voice of one crying out in the wilderness, 'Make straight the way of the Lord,'" as the prophet Isaiah said.

They asked him, "Why then are you baptizing if you are neither the Messiah, nor Elijah, nor the prophet?" John answered them, "I baptize with water. Among you stands one whom you do not know, the one who is coming after me; I am not worthy to untie the thong of his sandal." This took place in Bethany across the Jordan where John was baptizing.

The gospel of the Lord.

Overview
On this Sunday we part company with Mark to hear John the Evangelist tell us about the Baptist's role in presenting Jesus. The Baptist's role is defined sharply today. He is a forerunner, a herald.

John the Baptist is the shadow; Jesus the substance. John is the spokesperson; Jesus the big name. John is the witness; Jesus the central figure. John is the lamp; Jesus the light.

There is a palpable joy in today's liturgy. Jesus is the light, the joy, the song in our hearts. As we move nearer Christmas our enthusiasm for Jesus has an extra dimension. Our song of joy gathers pace as we savor the Christmas meeting with Jesus.

For the children we enlarge the portrait of Jesus (which is what this Sunday's gospel is essentially about) by listening (sometimes between the lines) to the testimony of John the Baptist.

Focusing Experiences

There is joy in the air today. Joy about Jesus. We create a mood of joy with colors, music, decorations, and words. We might pin up a headline like "Great Days of Joy Are Here!" at home or school. Joy is giving thanks to Jesus for being with us. Artists! Get to work before Sunday!

The Sunday's gospel describes how John's credentials are examined by a board of inquiry. We live in a world where the media are always carrying stories about investigating committees. Parents, teachers, and homilist will have no trouble explaining the mechanics of John the Baptist's appearance before the investigating committee.

Exploring the Word of God

This meeting of elders and priests was called to discuss John the Baptist and what he was up to at Bethany on the east side of the river Jordan. Let's follow the action!

"Assembled elders and priests, you have asked for my views," says one leader. "The facts are clear. He is in the desert. He has a big following. He is highly respected as a man of God. He is surrounded night and day by crowds of fans and well wishers. Half the people on the street where I live have gone out to meet him to get his blessing and hear his good news. And the news he has is about God's new days and God's new world. He says God's promise made to our ancestors is now to be fulfilled. What's wrong with that? He has won the hearts of the people. They say he makes sense.

"And another thing. He is so happy! It's unbelievable! He is full of joy with his good news that he says will change the world."

Another leader speaks up. "The difficulty about him is that we don't know who he is! We just don't know what standing he has with God. My proposal is that we send a delegation to talk to him—a face to face meeting. We need answers from him. We need to ask him who he is. Is he a prophet? Is he the great Elijah come back from God to be among us? Is he the Messiah of God? Messiah! I know it seems outrageous. Please don't be offended. I know that perhaps we shouldn't even think such a thing. But let us ask him and hear from his own mouth that he is not the Messiah. It will put all our minds at rest."

And so they sent a delegation to John the Baptist.

"John the Baptist, we are sent to ask you if you are the one promised by God to our people in ages past and now come among us as God's wonderful blessing on God's holy people? Are you the Messiah of God?"

"No!"

"If you are not the Messiah who are you, then? Are you Elijah?"

"Not Elijah! No."

"Then are you are the prophet sent from God on high to God's faithful people?"

12

"No!"

"Then tell us who you are. We have to take an answer back to the elders and priests who sent us. I see....You...are the voice of someone shouting in the desert, 'Make a straight path for the Lord to travel.'"

And the delegation returned to those who sent them.

"Here's the answer he gave us. It was a slogan. It was 'Make a straight path for the Lord to travel.' According to him—the way I understand his slogan—the great days of the Messiah are here. John the Baptist is calling on the people to prepare for the coming of the anointed one of God."

"Who do I think John the Baptist is? I think he sees himself as the herald, the announcer, the bearer of the good news that the Messiah can be expected at any moment. John is not making any claims about himself. He sees himself as a messenger for the Messiah."

This drama is unfolding. We haven't heard the end of it yet.

Call to Faith

Jesus is the light. John the Baptist is the witness to that light. He points out the light. We are called to welcome the light, but more—to be witnesses to the light. We are called to let his light shine in our lives, to let his light shine on the hidden darknesses in our lives—the weaknesses, the meannesses, the smallnesses—to bring out the goodness we are capable of.

Call to Action

Sing a song of welcome for Jesus. If this is during Mass, lead the children in singing it at the end of the homily.

Sing a song that celebrates Jesus as the light. You might use this song as the opening or closing song at Mass, or during the preparation of the gifts.

Invite someone from a voluntary Christian organization to give a witnessing word, as John did, to Jesus.

Interpret the puzzling call, "Make straight the way of the Lord." Help the children understand it. Ask them to express their interpretations in colorful drawings.

Fourth Sunday of Advent

Gospel
A reading from the holy Gospel according to Luke (1:26–38)

In the sixth month [of Elizabeth's pregnancy] the angel Gabriel was sent by God to a town in Galilee called Nazareth, to a virgin engaged to a man whose name was Joseph, of the house of David. The virgin's name was Mary. And he came to her and said, "Greetings, favored one! The Lord is with you." But she was much perplexed by his words and pondered what sort of greeting this might be. The angel said to her, "Do not be afraid, Mary, for you have found favor with God. And now, you will conceive in your womb and bear a son, and you will name him Jesus. He will be great, and will be called the Son of the Most High, and the Lord God will give to him the throne of his ancestor David. He will reign over the house of Jacob forever, and of his kingdom there will be no end." Mary said to the angel, "How can this be, since I am a virgin?" The angel said to her, "The Holy Spirit will come upon you, and the power of the Most High will overshadow you; therefore the child to be born will be holy; he will be called Son of God. And now, your relative Elizabeth in her old age has also conceived a son; and this is the sixth month for her who was said to be barren. For nothing will be impossible with God." Then Mary said, "Here am I, the servant of the Lord; let it be with me according to your word." Then the angel departed from her.

The gospel of the Lord.

Overview
On this Sunday the Evangelist Luke underlines the willing response of Mary to be the mother of the Messiah. The circumstances of her call are a profound spiritual experience for Mary. The significance of God's call and Mary's response is heightened by the introduction from the Jewish tradition of God's angel Gabriel, with whom Mary has a beautiful and gentle dialogue.

In the liturgy we pay a warm tribute to Mary in her role as mother-to-be of our Savior. It is the final action in our preparation for Christmas.

In bringing this gospel to the children, and in preaching the homily, we should try to keep alive the sense that this moment was, for Mary, a deeply personal encounter with God. To keep in tune with Mary's spiritual experience, we suggest a reflective approach, linked with experiences of children.

Focusing Experiences

Talk about people in the news or people you know who were chosen for a job of very special importance, of special delicacy. Help the children imagine their feelings of unease at being chosen for such an important task.

Talk about Mary, chosen to be mother of God's Son. Talk about Mary's feelings of devotion toward God. Talk about Mary, mother-to-be. Hang a picture of Mary in a prominent position at home during the week.

The homily in church might begin with a gentle and haunting solo song about the Virgin Mary.

Exploring the Word of God

(If possible, speak to the children against the backdrop of a wall hanging of Mary.)

You are a strange, wonderful girl, Mary. You are full of love. You loved God with a love that was strong and powerful and drew you close to God. You didn't want to ever be separated from God. You wanted a destiny with God. You wanted to reach out to God and be God's handmaid, God's cherished love.

It's in your eyes. It's in your heart. It was meant to be. A love born in heaven...a love that would light up your life.

You loved God with a joy that filled each day, and filled your life. You chose God as the love of your life. And God chose you to be the mother of the beloved Son.

In your dreams and in your visions you talked with God. You heard the voice of God's angel Gabriel, who brought God's message to you. You heard the angel because you were close to God. You were God's favored one. You weren't afraid of God's angel because you weren't afraid of God. Love drew you close to God to hear God's message.

You were ready and you were waiting to hear the angel's words because the angel brought you news from God—news to gladden your heart and deepen your love.

You heard God's angel tell you about a baby, a baby son you were going to bring to life as a gift to the world. A baby son that was to be your son and the Son of God.

You were chosen to be the mother of God's Son. You were chosen out of love to bring a gift of love to all those people who were waiting in hope for a message from their loving God. They were waiting with great expectation generation after generation for a message, a message not written in words that come out of the mouth, but a message of love in flesh and bone, a living life from God that would come out of your womb. You were chosen to carry Jesus for nine whole months in the comfort of your womb. You sheltered the Son of God and gave him life among us.

And you were willing—willing to be the handmaid of God, willing to bring God's love into the world, willing to bear God's Son.

Blessed are you among women and blessed is the fruit of your womb, Jesus.

Call to Faith
We grow in faith by paying a musical tribute to Mary with the solo/choral singing of the "Hail Mary" or the "Ave Maria."

Call to Action
Perhaps the children could compose a prayer or tribute to their own mothers who brought Jesus into our world for them. If this is done at Mass, do not do it as a brief introduction to the prayer of the faithful; instead, let it be a full two-three minute reflection after communion.

CHRISTMAS

Gospel
A reading from the holy Gospel according to Luke (2:1–14)

Joseph also went from the town of Nazareth in Galilee to Judea, to the city of David called Bethlehem, because he was descended from the house and family of David. He went to be registered with Mary, to whom he was engaged and who was expecting a child. While they were there, the time came for her to deliver her child. And she gave birth to her firstborn son and wrapped him in bands of cloth, and laid him in a manger, because there was no place for them in the inn.

In that region there were shepherds living in the fields, keeping watch over their flock by night. Then an angel of the Lord stood before them, and the glory of the Lord shone around them, and they were terrified. But the angel said to them, "Do not be afraid; for see—I am bringing you good news of great joy for all the people: to you is born this day in the city of David a Savior, who is the Messiah, the Lord. This will be a sign for you: you will find a child wrapped in bands of cloth and lying in a manger." And suddenly there was with the angel a multitude of the heavenly host, praising God and saying,

"Glory to God in the highest
heaven,
and on earth peace among
those whom he favors!"

The gospel of the Lord.

Overview
Jesus is born into our world. The details are woven into the nativity story. The Scripture themes are glory, wonder, praise, and excitement.

He is with us, among us—the Savior, the Lord. God has visited God's people! Glory and praise to God for this great and wonderful day! *Gloria in excelsis Deo!*

The liturgy shouts out in exuberant praise and celebration. Our churches echo to the sound of Christmas songs.

The children can be introduced effectively to this gospel passage in the context of the crèche. We weave our own kind of celebration around the Christmas story.

Focusing Experiences
Ask the children to visit the crèche in advance. Let them help to put the pieces in place. Encourage parents at home to set up a crèche. Talk about why you place the figures in the positions you finally give them.

Exploring the Word of God
(Delivered near the crèche)
Mary, we see you standing by the manger. You are with Jesus, your baby. And Joseph is there, to make things good for you and the baby Jesus.

Mother of Jesus, you walked with Joseph to Bethlehem. Your baby was about to be born. It was a long road. And there was no room in the inn. That was a shock for you, and a worry.

The stable offered you shelter and some kind of welcome. The cattle and the sheep are near you. They keep you warm. They almost seem part of your family. They seem very easy and at home with you.

It looks cozy with the straw on the ground and everything so clean. It probably wasn't cozy or clean like that. But we hope it was a good place to be. It was good because you were there with your baby, the Savior king. And you brought him into this world to help us find a good way to live and grow.

And the shepherds came rushing in. Weren't you amazed when you saw the look of wonder in their eyes? Were you embarrassed when they knelt before you and the baby Jesus? Did you wonder what it all meant? They were good men. They knew what was happening. They knew that God had come among the people. They were so thankful they couldn't stop praising God. It was good for you to have them there. They were company for you.

Mary, you are a mother to Jesus and a mother to us.

Our Mother, we pray to you. We look to you for comfort. We look to you for love. We know you understand us. We know we can talk to you and tell you things. We know our worries are important to you. We know you are on our side, listening with a mother's love.

Call to Faith
Mary and Joseph and Jesus, you are all welcome into our crib, into our church, into our homes, into our hearts on this happy Christmas Day.

18

Call to Action

Sing Christmas songs and carols at every opportunity in class or during the Mass.

Encourage the children to write letters to their mothers, thanking them especially for encouraging them to be good. Have them decorate an "I love you" card to their mothers.

Have them write a letter to Mary saying they understand how she feels and how glad they are that she chose to be the mother of God's Son.

Holy Family

Gospel
A reading from the holy Gospel according to Luke (2:22–40)

Now there was a man in Jerusalem whose name was Simeon; this man was righteous and devout, looking forward to the consolation of Israel, and the Holy Spirit rested on him. It had been revealed to him by the Holy Spirit that he would not see death before he had seen the Lord's Messiah. Guided by the Spirit, Simeon came into the temple; and when the parents brought in the child Jesus, to do for him what was customary under the law, Simeon took him in his arms and praised God, saying,
"Master, now you are dismissing
your servant in peace,
according to your word;
for my eyes have seen your
salvation,
which you have prepared in
the presence of all
peoples,
a light for revelation to the
Gentiles
and for glory to your people
Israel."
There was also a prophet, Anna. She was of a great age, having lived to the age of eighty-four. She never left the temple but worshiped there with fasting and prayer night and day. At that moment she came, and began to praise God and to speak about the child to all who were looking for the redemption of Jerusalem.

The gospel of the Lord.

Overview
It was entirely appropriate that the Lord should be greeted by representatives of the prophets (Simeon and Anna) when he entered his temple. It was fitting that Simeon and Anna should be called on to fulfill

this task, because their experience of God and God's ways was second to none. It was fitting in the cause of the dignity of women that one of those called to introduce Jesus of Nazareth to the public was Anna.

From a celebration of the family of Jesus, Mary, and Joseph, the liturgy today pays tribute to the Christian family, that kernel and cradle of faith and hope.

I suggest that if the personalities of Simeon and Anna are enlarged, then their witness to Jesus will be more memorable. It should also be noted that by paying tribute to these two likeable, warm, and striking personalities we are paying a tribute to the wisdom and good sense of an age group that includes our grandparents and the older generation.

Focusing Experiences
An introductory tribute to the wisdom of parents and grandparents. They might even be credited with seeing more deeply into things than we might have imagined.

Exploring the Word of God
He was an old man and a good man—perhaps like our grandfathers. He was very good humored. He had plenty of stories and was a great storyteller. You never knew until the end of the story how it was going to work out. There was nearly always a surprise toward the end. Simeon had stories about kings and princesses, about farmers and sailors, about champions and brave women, about children and evil spirits, about people possessed by the devil and going crazy to worship false gods, about journeys into faraway lands and cruel kings, about escaping from a land of sin in the middle of the night. He had a great following. People came on visits to his house just to hear his stories.

People agreed he was a holy man. He spent a lot of time around God's temple. He said he felt at home there. He said he felt peace there. He said that was what gave him his happiness. He said that was where the stories came to him.

He had the air of a man who talked sense about God. He seemed to know what God was up to. People said he was a prophet, a man who had the wisdom of God in him. Maybe that was carrying it too far. But he was certainly a man close to God.

When he saw Mary and Joseph and the child Jesus, he just lit up. He couldn't be stopped. His face became radiant. His voice broke into a joyful shout. People stood still to hear what he was saying. He looked strong and imposing there before the people, his white beard flowing down to his chest. His old age gave him a look of authority and strength. People gathered around him afraid to miss what he was saying. He began to make a speech. He raised his hands for silence and the crowd hushed. He said he had an announcement to make. He stood close to Mary, who held the child Jesus. He turned to the mother and her child and welcomed them with rich and flowing words. But it was no ordinary welcome. It was a welcome fit for kings and saviors. It was a welcome for God's child. It was a welcome tailor-made for new times and a new age. Gently he took the child Jesus in his arms and cradled the baby to his heart.

He raised his head and his arms to heaven and thanked the Lord for letting him live to see this day and this baby with his own eyes. He said, "I have seen the Savior. He will be a light to lead the people to a new life, and he will be a beacon light to bring God's people into new times and new days. Now I can die in peace. My happiness is complete."

Not far away in another part of the temple was Anna, an old and kindly lady who was much respected for her goodness and wisdom. People said that in the things to do with God she understood more than any living soul. She was always around the temple praying and talking to God. When the days of fasting came she could go without food for hours and hours.

She came by just at that moment and, like the old man Simeon, was transfixed by the sight of the baby. She stood in total silence, rooted to the ground like a statue, her eyes wide open and staring in amazement at the baby. She came to herself and raised her arms before the people and called for silence. With her voice trembling with excitement she pointed out, for all to see, the baby sent by God to God's people to lead them into new and glorious times.

It was a marvelous sight seeing the two old people, Simeon and Anna, making the speeches of their lives and doing it so well to an audience they captivated.

People who knew them both took what they said very much to heart and went away praising God. They wondered about the baby and his mother, and they talked with excitement in their voices about the new times that God was giving to their people.

Call to Faith

We pay tribute to the family of Mary, Joseph, and their infant Jesus. We ask them to keep our own family in their care.

We pay tribute to Simeon and Anna, and everyone from an older generation whose heritage we have received and whose advice and wisdom can make a difference to us.

We welcome Jesus into our hearts and into our homes.

Call to Action

Welcome the older generation who have come to celebrate this Mass with the children and their parents.

Ask an elderly parishioner whom the children respect to deliver a two-minute story/reflection/prayer. This can be done during the homily or as a post-communion reflection.

Arrange a family day of prayer for several families in your neighborhood.

Help the children to:

Make a plan to go on a family outing.

Have a family fast for a circle of families.

Visit old people of their acquaintance.

Prepare a treat for older friends.

Arrange a liturgy to celebrate their extended families.

Second Sunday After Christmas

Gospel
A reading from the holy Gospel according to John (1:1,3–5,10,14)

In the beginning was the Word, and the Word was with God, and the Word was God. All things came into being through him, and the life was the light of all people. The light shines in the darkness, and the darkness did not overcome it.

He was in the world; yet the world did not know him.

And the Word became flesh and lived along us, and we have seen his glory, the glory as of a father's only son, full of grace and truth.

The gospel of the Lord.

Overview
We have seen Jesus in the manger and we have celebrated. He is the voice of God come among us. But the image of the baby in the manger must give way to the image of Jesus our Savior, the risen Jesus, Jesus the Lord.

John's gospel stands back from the manger and pays a tribute to Jesus who is the Word of God for everyone, everywhere. As John leads the adults into a reflection on the place of Jesus in the sweep of history, we can also lead the children into a reflection on who Jesus is for them today.

Exploring the Word of God
Today we ask the children to remember the gospel story of Jesus and the children. The details... the talk between the mothers and the disciples... how Jesus blessed the children.

We ask the children to imagine that they are in that group of children on that day. Their mothers are there. Jesus blesses them. It is a good feeling being near Jesus.

Imagine another scene. You are standing with the centurion at the foot of the cross. The centurion is saying to you, "This surely was the Son of God." You ask him what he means...

And finally you go with the women to the tomb. It is empty! Jesus is risen from the dead! You rush back to tell Peter and the others. A little later in the company of the disciples you meet the risen Jesus. And you feel great joy.

Call to Faith

You are Jesus our friend.

    You are Jesus our Savior.

    You are the risen Jesus.

    You are the Word made flesh.

    We meet you at this Mass.

    We hear your Word.

    We give thanks to God for everything you are to us, and everything you do for us.

    We eat the bread of life and we come close to you.

    You are our friend, Savior, Lord, today and always, for ever and ever.

Call to Action

Decorate some banners with the titles of Jesus the Lord or Jesus our Savior. Use them in the church and carry them during the processions of the liturgy.

    Sing songs of praise to the risen Jesus.

EPIPHANY

Gospel
A reading from the holy Gospel according to Matthew (2:1–12)

In the time of King Herod, after Jesus was born in Bethlehem of Judea, wise men from the East came to Jerusalem, asking, "Where is the child who has been born king of the Jews? For we observed his star at its rising, and have come to do him homage."

When they had heard the king, they set out; and there, ahead of them, went the star that they had seen at its rising, until it stopped over the place where the child was. When they saw that the star had stopped, they were overwhelmed with joy. On entering the house, they saw the child with Mary his mother; and they knelt down and paid him homage. Then, opening their treasure chests, they offered him gifts of gold, frankincense, and myrrh. And having been warned in a dream not to return to Herod, they left for their own country by another road.

The gospel of the Lord.

Overview
There is a focus in today's gospel on the strangers from the East who came to worship Jesus. The story steams straight ahead into the rights of strangers to receive and worship Jesus. This might not have gone down well in some quarters at the time, but the point has to be made that Jesus is not Savior to any "in" group. No color or race has a God-given right to claim God's Messiah as their own. He is Savior to all. This is today's story and today's underlying message.

When the children are present today there is an opportunity to express solidarity with minority groups. Efforts should be made to give some visible expression to our solidarity around the manger with minority groups with whom the children can identify.

Focusing Experiences
Discuss some poems or songs that explore the feelings of strangers, foreigners, outsiders, newcomers.

Ask parents and children to talk at home about the feelings of minority groups in their community.

Exploring the Word of God

They were strangers, these wise men from the East. Strangers on a mission. They were looking for their Savior. Because they were strangers the search was more difficult. Strangers are often treated with suspicion. But they were guided by a star. King Herod tried to use them to trap the infant Jesus, but they saw through his conspiracy and had no more dealings with him.

They kept up the search and found Jesus in the stable. They knelt before their Savior and gave him gold, frankincense, and myrrh—gifts from wise men to their Lord and king.

Call to Faith

Gentle Savior, we are the people of the world.

We come from every nation under heaven. We live in the north, the south, the east, and the west. In one place we are at home. In another place we are strangers and foreigners. Lord Jesus, we feel at home with you.

Our skins are colored. We are white. We are black. We are brown. Our color makes us feel at home in one place. In another place we are made to feel odd. We are made to feel like outsiders. Lord Jesus, we don't feel odd with you.

Our language is different. In one place it is the local language. In another when we speak, it makes people feel uneasy. We feel we don't belong. We are strangers. Lord Jesus, we never feel uneasy with you.

We are rich. We are poor. We who are poor feel the rich couldn't care less about us. We who are rich feel the poor have only themselves to blame. Lord Jesus, rich or poor you welcome us.

Call to Action

This is an opportunity to express the diversity of people and cultures in the parish. It is an opportunity to give a voice and a welcome to minority groups. It is a time to hear Jesus welcomed in minority languages, in minority songs.

At Mass, give space and time to outsiders (at the introduction, penitential rite, homily, prayer of the faithful, communion reflection)

We must gather various traditions around the manger as one family of worshipers.

Consider sending a small delegation of worshipers to the church of another Christian tradition at this time, and welcome a group of worshipers from their church to sing a song of welcome to Jesus with you.

Baptism of the Lord

Gospel
A reading from the holy Gospel according to Mark (1:7–11)

In those days Jesus came from Nazareth of Galilee and was baptized by John in the Jordan. And just as he was coming up out of the water, he saw the heavens torn apart and the Spirit descending like a dove on him. And a voice came from heaven, "You are my Son, the Beloved; with you I am well pleased."

The gospel of the Lord.

Overview
It's the beginning of Jesus' ministry. He is called out of a quiet life in Nazareth. He is set apart and commissioned to do God's work.

Focusing Experiences
The call of Jesus could be given a rich context if we encourage a parent to talk to the children about the call to parenthood.

Exploring the Word of God
People were at the Jordan river. John the Baptist was baptizing, and people were coming and going. Then Jesus came forward for baptism. He had come from Nazareth. He was a stranger. No one else knew him, but John knew him. And John knew that the Spirit of God was in Jesus. John baptized Jesus, and as soon as Jesus was baptized a voice was heard from the heavens saying, "You are my son, the beloved, my favor rests on you."

Jesus was anointed by God for his mission at that moment. He was picked out by God, set apart, chosen, anointed. He left the Jordan and soon took the road toward the towns and villages nearby.

(What did it feel like for Jesus? What were his fears and worries as he set off to say his first words in public? What was he going to say? Why was he doing it?)

Call to Faith
Jesus, you were called out of Nazareth to walk a new path.

Jesus, you were called out of Nazareth to be the voice of God to the people.

Jesus, you were called out of Nazareth to take a hard road, to face opposition, to meet disappointments.

But you faced the road because you heard the call of God and answered it.

Jesus, each of us is called in baptism to walk with you as your disciple.

We have our own roads to walk.

We are called out of our own homes, out of our own streets, out of our own neighborhoods to be part of the world where we make time for God and for our friends.

Jesus, we hear the call of God. We are ready to face the road. Be with us every step of the way.

Call to Action

What is it like to be called to be a parent? Is it about giving and receiving love? Is it about passing on values that come from Jesus? Encourage a parent to say a few words to the children about what it means to be called to be a Christian parent.

There are plenty of songs about the call of Jesus. We can express our faith by singing such a song now.

First Sunday of Lent

Gospel
A reading from the holy Gospel according to Mark (1:12–15)

And the Spirit immediately drove him out into the wilderness. He was in the wilderness forty days, tempted by Satan; and he was with the wild beasts; and the angels waited on him.

Now after John was arrested, Jesus came to Galilee, proclaiming the good news of God, and saying, "The time is fulfilled, and the kingdom of God has come near; repent, and believe in the good news."

The gospel of the Lord.

Overview
Jesus' vocation is to combat evil, to overcome evil, to bring to the world salvation from the forces of evil. It's his life's work. This struggle against evil will be the hallmark of his ministry. In today's gospel story he is engaged in his first pitched battle against evil in a wilderness—where the devil roams. The battle is won, and this first hard-won victory over evil buys Jesus the right to begin preaching God's saving word to the people.

In today's liturgy, we are called to make our own fight against evil, to do combat against evil, to win victory in our own trials and tribulations.

For the children we enlarge the inner struggle that Jesus faced. It should help the children to see something of the inner turmoil of all temptations. His victory is all the more memorable because of the intensity of the battle inside his mind and imagination.

Focusing Experiences
Parents and teachers can survey a variety of classical music records to discover a piece that captures the mood of desolation. This choice of music will provide the setting for the gospel story of this Sunday. Discuss with the children why this music is appropriate to the gospel.

A more immediate focus for the homily might center on thoughts of home as a place where one hears comforting noises—sounds of traffic, machinery, people, people talking, music, radio, television, perhaps even a clock striking the hour. At night one falls asleep to familiar sounds.

Exploring the Word of God

Where Jesus went there were no familiar sounds. It was empty. It was lonely—no beauty, no flowers, no growth, no noises to mark the time. They called it a wilderness because it was a dead place. It was deathly quiet in a way that was eerie, ghostly, frightening.

Jesus could hear himself breathing. He could hear his heart beating in his ribs. He was walking into a place that was so quiet that it seemed some evil presence had shut out every warm, homely sound. It was a place where the devil was said to live. Jesus knew what he was up against. It was him and the devil. He had to first face the devil. If he survived that contest with honor, then he could face the people in God's name to bring them the good news.

When he went a short distance into this lifeless place the devil put his eye on him and transfixed him with his evil power. The devil filled Jesus' mind with exciting dreams. Under the power of the devil the dreams unfolded before him to reveal a world so rich and so wonderful and so exciting that it took Jesus' breath away. But he didn't give in. He didn't say "yes." He held back. He held his ground.

The world of dreams and magic danced around him. He wanted to dance to the music of the dream, but how could he speak to the people in God's name if he danced to the tune of the devil's music? The devil's dream-world swirled around him inviting him to be king, king over everybody, over every living thing. King of the world! Every star in the universe would be his. But—and this was to be the price—he would have to become best friends with the devil. He who stood for God— best friends with the devil!

His body ached. It was like a fever. His mind was in a turmoil. He knew he stood for God. That mattered. That mattered a lot. That was all that mattered. The rest had to be resisted. The dream? No! The music? No! The vision of kingly greatness? No! No! No!

With a mighty "No!" he seemed to break through to a world of gentle noises, a world of life, of familiar sounds. A few animals sat near him keeping him company. He felt comforted by God and in God's presence.

When he rested he felt ready to go and talk to the people in God's name.

Call to Faith

Jesus, you resisted. It took all your strength and all your energy. You held out because you love God.

You were alone as dreams of greatness and glory swirled around you, enticing you to turn your back on God and go the devil's way. You said no. You did it for yourself. You did it for God, and you did it for us. We thank you and we praise you for saying no.

We are called to carry on our own fight against evil.

We are called to resist temptation.

We are called to be led by Jesus, to walk with Jesus in our struggles and temptations.

Call to Action

Find words now to comfort Jesus after his temptation.

Take time to firm up on lenten resolutions.

During the week have a public hour of Christian renewal with songs, readings, poems, and speeches.

Make arrangements to attend the sacrament of reconciliation.

Encourage parents and children to have a family fast.

Encourage the children to do drawings of the great encounter between Jesus and the devil in this desolate place.

Second Sunday of Lent

Gospel
A reading from the holy Gospel according to Mark (9:2–10)

Jesus took with him Peter and James and John, and led them up a high mountain apart, by themselves. And he was transfigured before them, and his clothes became dazzling white, such as no one on earth could bleach them. And there appeared to them Elijah and Moses, who were talking with Jesus. Then Peter said to Jesus, "Rabbi, it is good for us to be here; let us make three dwellings, one for you, one for Moses, and one for Elijah." He did not know what to say, for they were terrified. Then a cloud overshadowed them, and from the cloud there came a voice, "This is my Son, the Beloved; listen to him!" Suddenly when they looked around, they saw no one with them any more, but only Jesus.

The gospel of the Lord.

Overview
Mark's story today is one of blessing and light, a vision to strengthen and console us. All too soon we will see Jesus laid low in Gethsemane. Today we get a glimpse of his glory.

The liturgy keeps pace with the Scripture. We are sustained in our lenten efforts by the experience of light and blessing.

We do our best, in a matter-of-fact sort of way, to lead the children into the vision that the disciples experienced on the mountain and which gave them heart to face future tribulations. We point up this transfiguration experience to help the children see Jesus the man, in glory.

Focusing Experiences
Ask the children to remember a time when they were on a mountain with their parents. Have them talk about the experience. Have them imagine the mountain as a place of quiet, of retreat, where holy people might go to pray in magnificent surroundings. Ask them to imagine how people long ago felt close to God high up on a mountain as their heads reached into the clouds and as they surveyed the sweep of the world that spread out before them.

The immediate focus for the homily might center around the thought that mountains have always been regarded as special places—places of visions and dreams and ideas, and where people find peace to talk to God. Holy men and women often went to the top of a mountain to speak with God. Pilgrims often climb a holy mountain to pray and sing and come close to God. Mountains seem a good place to clear out your mind and find space for God. Monasteries have been founded and built on top of mountains because they seemed good places for holy people to be in touch with God. Croagh Patrick in Ireland is a holy mountain that pilgrims climb each year to make good intentions, ask God's favors, and receive the blessings that go with the pilgrimage.

Exploring the Word of God

Jesus asked Peter, James, and John to go up the mountain with him. They knew that something big was up. They walked into the foothills and began to trudge their way up the mountain. After a time they seemed to be above the world and alone. There and then, quite suddenly, their eyes were opened to a vision. They saw Jesus in a way they had never seen him before. He was as different as you could imagine—really changed! He was transfigured into a God-like figure: dazzling, almost transparent. Beside him stood the figures of Moses and Elijah, the great men of history and the heroes of the holy books. Peter wanted to build three covered dwellings where Jesus and these two great heroes from the past could be honored. But it was clear that all the honor on the day was to be for Jesus. A voice from heaven said, "This is my Son, the beloved, listen to him." Peter, James, and John knew that God was talking to them in their hearts about who Jesus really was.

The vision disappeared, and the three disciples stood on the bleak and windswept mountain with Jesus. He was as he always was and no different. But they knew something about him now that they wouldn't forget. It was crystal clear to them that Jesus and God were connected, closely connected. That was the message of the vision. That's what they learned. Jesus had the backing of God. Jesus was God's choice for God's work among the people. Those who followed Jesus would be following God. And this thought filled them with courage. They never felt better. It was a boost to their confidence. It filled them with hope.

Jesus turned to them and said, "Say nothing about what you saw today to anyone. The meaning will become clear when the time is right." They made their way down the mountain with Jesus and continued on their journey.

Call to Faith

We see Jesus in his glory. We can feel confidence with him just as the disciples did.

Call to Action

This is a time for song. We have seen Jesus in his glory. It is a time to sing the praises of Jesus.

Our liturgy could do with a resounding expression of faith in Jesus. Invite the school band with drums and trumpets to lead a short procession around the church.

Give the children time to renew lenten resolutions with new heart and new determination.

Ask the children to draw Jesus in his glory.

We have seen Jesus in his glory. It is time to say the praises of Jesus in a litany. Help the children compose a litany in praise of Jesus.

THIRD SUNDAY OF LENT

Gospel
A reading from the holy Gospel according to John (2:13–17)

The Passover of the Jews was near, and Jesus went up to Jerusalem. In the temple he found people selling cattle, sheep, and doves, and the money changers seated at their tables. Making a whip of cords, he drove all of them out of the temple, both the sheep and the cattle. He also poured out the coins of the money changers and overturned their tables. He told those who were selling the doves, "Take these things out of here! Stop making my Father's house a marketplace!" His disciples remembered that it was written, "Zeal for your house will consume me."

The gospel of the Lord.

Overview
In today's reading Jesus is claiming a special place in his people's sacred history by clearing the traders out the temple. He is doing what the prophets and the holy books said the Messiah would do. He is letting those who have ears to hear and eyes to see know that the new age, the messianic times, have dawned.

The liturgy alerts us to the new ways and the new challenges that Jesus proposes. We must change and grow.

Business in the temple enclosure is brought to a halt by the man from Nazareth. For the children, we let this exciting story find its own level, but hint at the deeper meaning.

Focusing Experiences
Parents and teachers, let your imagination roam free and create a story of a beggarwoman or beggarman who is recognized to be the true queen or king.

Ask the children to think about:

Fables, stories from books and television

• the shock when the true heir appears

• the shock when a long-lost child is recognized to be a son or daughter

• the shock when a beggarman is revealed as the king

Exploring the Word of God

Jesus does something that holy prophets down the centuries said the Messiah would do. Here is the story...

Some people were buying animals. Some people were selling animals. Some were changing foreign money into local currency. There was a smell of blood, a smell of animals, the din of business, and the hustle and bustle of people doing deals and making money. And this was happening in the temple enclosure, in the holy place. Jesus surveyed all that was happening—the rows of stalls and the crowds of people. It offended him. It was an outrage. Jesus felt driven by the Spirit to make a stand against this abuse.

He cracked a whip over their heads and made a fiery speech. "Shame on you who turn my Father's house into a bazaar. Shame on you who bring the smell of animals into this holy place. Shame on you who soil this holy ground with your stalls and your wares. My Father's house is a place of prayer and you defile it with deals and bargains. Out with you from this holy place."

He said a lot more besides, and the traders and money changers took notice. He seemed to mean business. The traders took to heart what he was saying and moved away.

Others who listened to him were angry because they saw a deep meaning in his actions. What he did was what the holy books said God's Messiah would do one day. Through his actions of clearing the temple he was doing the work of the Messiah. That really raised a buzz of anger. How could Jesus be the Messiah? Such a thought, they said, was outrageous, intolerable. They got very angry at the idea.

For his friends and followers, what was done on this day was yet more evidence that Jesus was God's beloved Son, his chosen one, and yes, the Messiah of God. And they were happy to follow him into the new ways that God was revealing to God's people.

Call to Faith

We are called to accept Jesus as our Messiah, our leader—the one given to us by God.

Call to Action

Sing a song of faith in Jesus the Messiah.

Review lenten resolutions. Make adjustments. Drop some resolutions. Think about what God really wants from us (mention this during the penitential rite at Mass).

Here is a suggestion for a post-communion meditation:

Lord Jesus, many didn't recognize you. They felt uncomfortable.
Jesus, bread of life, you are hidden from us. We feel a little un-

comfortable, a little uncertain. But we hear your words. We hear you appeal to us to love one another. We see you with the eyes of faith. We see you, Lord Jesus, our Messiah, the voice of God among us.

In class, give the children a chance to dramatize the story of the clearing of the temple. The interpretation of the action is significant, so give a role to an observer who interprets the action. Or use two observers—one who is opposed to Jesus, another who is sympathetic and sees the revelation of the Messiah in his actions that day.

Fourth Sunday of Lent

Gospel
(For pastoral reasons the gospel reading for year A has been chosen)
A reading from the holy Gospel according to John (9:1–41)

As Jesus walked along, he saw a man blind from birth. He spat on the ground and made mud with the saliva and spread the mud on the man's eyes, saying to him, "Go, wash in the pool of Siloam." Then he went and washed and came back able to see. The neighbors and those who had seen him before as a beggar began to ask, "Is this not the man who used to sit and beg?" Some were saying, "It is he." Others were saying, "No, but it is someone like him." He kept saying, "I am the man."

They brought to the Pharisees the man who had formerly been blind. Now it was a sabbath day when Jesus made the mud and opened his eyes. Then the Pharisees also began to ask him how he had received his sight. He said to them, "He put mud on my eyes. Then I washed, and now I see." Some of the Pharisees said, "This man is not from God, for he does not observe the sabbath." But others said, "How can a man who is a sinner perform such signs?" And they were divided. So they said again to the blind man, "What do you say about him? It was your eyes he opened." He said, "He is a prophet."

The gospel of the Lord.

Overview
This story introduces Jesus in a dramatic way. He reaches out in compassion to the blind man. Yet he faces opposition. People are struggling to come to terms with who he is.

The children's liturgy today and every family Mass presumes a willingness on the part of parents to play a role. Those parents who have a talent for it should be invited today to stand at a microphone and play a role in the radio piece below (from *The Columba Lectionary for Masses with Children*) about the cure of the blind man. It will enlarge the portrait of Jesus for the children.

Focusing Experiences

Parents and teacher can help children understand the various kinds of blindness.

Physical—doesn't see with the eyes.

Spiritual—doesn't see with the soul; doesn't see Jesus.

Moral—doesn't see with the heart; doesn't see evil, hunger, injustice.

Exploring the Word of God

(Option 1)

Blind man	I was blind. He cured me.
Interviewer	Were you really blind, totally blind?
Blind man	Blind as a bat. My parents and all my neighbors are witnesses to that.
Interviewer	How could Jesus of Nazareth do such a thing for you?
Blind man	He's a prophet. He's a man of God.
Interviewer	The authorities don't share your high opinion of him. They say he is making a nuisance of himself. They say he's good at gathering crowds and making empty promises.
Blind man	Empty promises! He gave me my sight!
Interviewer	He has power to cure. That's what you are saying?
Blind man	He has power from God.
Interviewer	Power from God?
Blind man	What happened to me was a sign from God for all the people to see.
Interviewer	A sign of what?
Blind man	A sign of who Jesus is. He's the chosen one of God. He's the Messiah. He is the one who is to come.
Interviewer	If that is so, why are the authorities in the temple, who know all about these things, saying that he's a fake?
Blind man	Our people have been waiting down the years and down the centuries for God's anointed one to come among us. We are always on the lookout for signs of his coming. My cure was such a sign. A marvelous sign for me and for all the people who live in hope. The authorities have lost their nerve. They don't seem to recognize signs that stare them in the face. It's very sad.
Interviewer	Sir, you're from the temple. Is Jesus the anointed one?
Official	Out of the question! The blind man is carried away by whatever relief the man from Nazareth gave him.
Interviewer	He was blind. Now he can see.
Official	That's in some doubt.
Interviewer	In doubt? His parents say he was blind from birth.
Official	We spoke to his parents. At first they said he was blind

	from birth but when we cross-examined them closely they became confused and uncertain. They didn't stick to their story.
Interviewer	They are poor, uneducated people. You are men of words. Did you not confuse them?
Official	All we are saying is that Jesus of Nazareth did not cure the blind man. The cure was not a sign from God. The anointed one is not among us. Jesus of Nazareth must not be believed. Jesus of Nazareth cannot be the anointed one.
Interviewer	Why?
Official	It's our business to watch for God's signs and examine them. Anything Jesus of Nazareth has done is not even worth looking at. Everything about him is wrong. Most of all he doesn't seem to have any regard for Moses, our greatest prophet. That's a real giveaway. No, there's nothing about Jesus of Nazareth that we could recommend to the people.
Blind man	They can say what they like. I, and thousands more like me, say different. When Jesus of Nazareth cured me I knelt down before him and I worshiped him. I worshiped him. That's what I think of him.

(Option 2)

The man was blind. Not just sort of blind but really blind. He couldn't see a thing. It was darkness for him day and night. It was always the same, darkness since his birth.

Jesus cured him and gave him his sight. The man who was blind could see. This caused mayhem, chaos, and arguments. Some people who didn't believe in Jesus wanted to know what he was playing at. "If he thinks he is God's Messiah or God's holy messenger we will soon put a stop to that." Others said: "We believe in him. We truly believe in him." That started the arguments all over again. Jesus became a hero for those who believed in him and an enemy for others who didn't believe in him.

"He cured the blind man," his supporters and followers said. "That is a sign that Jesus has God's power. If you listen to him you are listening to God."

"That's rubbish," the others said. "The blind man was never blind at all. It was a set-up. A fix! Only the foolish and the gullible follow Jesus."

With that, the man who was once blind and now could see came back to Jesus. He fell at Jesus feet and with tears in his eyes said: "I believe."

41

Call to Faith

Jesus, we believe in you.

>We believe you are the Lord.

>We believe you are our Savior.

>We believe you are the Living God.

>We believe you have the words of life.

>Help us to see and appreciate the good things in our lives.

>Help us to see the needs of others.

>Help us to see or own afflictions and troubles as an opportunity to understand other people's hurts and troubles.

Call to Action

We have to be careful with this gospel story, or any Scripture story that makes metaphorical connections between a physical disability and a spiritual or moral disability. It's easy for children to get the idea that physical blindness is "bad." This can increase misunderstandings and prejudice against blind people. Ask a blind parishioner to speak to the children about blindness and to bear testimony to the new ways of seeing that blindness has brought to him or her.

Help the children ask for forgiveness for failure to see the needs of others.

In a post-communion reflection ask God to open our eyes to see Jesus in the bread of life.

In class, dramatize the story of the blind man's encounter with Jesus.

FIFTH SUNDAY OF LENT

Gospel
A reading from the holy Gospel according to John (12:20–33)

Jesus said, "Very truly, I tell you, unless a grain of wheat falls into the earth and dies, it remains just a single grain; but if it dies, it bears much fruit.

"Now my soul is troubled. And what should I say— 'Father, save me from this hour'? No, it is for this reason that I have come to this hour. Father, glorify your name." Then a voice came from heaven, "I have glorified it, and I will glorify it again."

The gospel of the Lord.

Overview
The time for Jesus' passion has come. He is afraid of death, yet he beckons it. The grain of wheat must die to produce a rich harvest. The liturgy leaves us in no doubt that death to sin gives way to a rich Christian life. This must be our pattern and style.

We want to give the children a sense of the inner turmoil that the thought of death provokes in Jesus, and the rewards he considers his death could bring to us.

Focusing Experiences
Parents and teachers can take children out into a garden or into the fields and point out all the signs of new life in Spring.

How can death, with all its negative qualities, have a redeeming positive side? What does nature teach us? That life follows death. That death, despite the darkness and blackness of winter, is transformed into life.

Other thoughts about death might arise—for example, a story of someone who dies to save another.

Exploring the Word of God
Some Greeks who came to Jerusalem wished to be introduced to Jesus and made themselves known to the disciples. The disciples spoke to Jesus and explained that a group of Greeks, strangers and foreigners, wished to speak to him.

"I cannot do anything for them," Jesus said. "I have to die first."

He said, "I have to die," so casually, so calmly, that they were shocked and stunned.

"Yes," he went on, "death will release me. I have to face it. The seed in the ground dies to grow to new life. In death I will bring a rich salvation to many."

Such talk disturbed them. They tried to change the conversation, but he persisted.

"I must face death. I could ask the Father to save me from passion and death. It must not be so. My hour has come."

The disciples could see the torment in his eyes at the prospect of death. They could see the worry written on his face. Jesus raised his eyes to heaven as if to put himself into the care of his heavenly Father. People heard what sounded to some like a clap of thunder. Others heard the voice of angels comforting Jesus. Jesus himself heard the voice of God blessing him for what he was about to do for all humankind.

Call to Faith

Jesus, our Savior, you faced death to free us.

You faced death to give us life.

You faced death to become new life for us.

You faced death to bring new life to all people.

You faced death to make us sons and daughters of God.

Jesus, our Savior, we thank you, we praise you, we glorify you.

Call to Action

This is a time to give thanks to Jesus for all that his sacrifice means to us.

It is a time for quiet music as we comfort and thank him (as the above Call to Faith section is read).

Encourage the children to be with Jesus in a quiet place as he contemplates the prospect of his death. This might be a few minutes spent this week in the presence of the Blessed Sacrament.

Encourage families to gather around the crucifix and to say the kind of litany used in the Call to Faith.

PASSION SUNDAY

Gospel
The Passion according to Mark (14:1–15:47)

Then the soldiers led him into the courtyard of the palace (that is, the governor's headquarters); and they called together the whole cohort. And they clothed him in a purple cloak; and after twisting some thorns into a crown, they put it on him. And they began saluting him, "Hail, King of the Jews!" They stuck his head with a reed, spat upon him, and knelt down in homage to him. After mocking him, they stripped him of the purple cloak and put his own clothes on him. Then they led him out to crucify him.

They compelled a passer-by, who was coming in from the country, to carry his cross; it was Simon of Cyrene, the father of Alexander and Rufus. Then they brought Jesus to the place called Golgotha (which means the place of a skull).

Now at the festival [Pilate] used to release a prisoner for them, anyone for whom they asked. Now a man called Barabbas was in prison with the rebels who had committed murder during the insurrection. So the crowd came and began to ask Pilate to do for them according to his custom. Then he answered them, "Do you want me to release for you the King of the Jews?" For he realized that it was out of jealousy that the chief priests had handed him over. But the chief priests stirred up the crowd to have him release Barabbas for them instead. "Then what do you wish me to do with the man you call the King of the Jews?" They shouted back, "Crucify him!" Pilate asked them, "Why, what evil has he done?" But they shouted all the more, "Crucify him!" So Pilate, wishing to satisfy the crowd, released Barabbas for them; and after flogging Jesus, he handed him over to be crucified.

Now when the centurion, who stood facing him, saw that in this way he breathed his last, he said, "Truly this man was God's Son!"

The gospel of the Lord.

Overview

Jesus' death on the cross stands for his absolute, unlimited, totally self-less giving of his life in love for us. On Passion Sunday we focus on that belief and pay honor to the Savior who gave himself lovingly in death for us.

In the passion narrative we listen to the details of a life given with unbounded love. The passion of Jesus is a long drama carefully worked out by Mark. A series of plots and sub-plots are presented. The action revolves around Jesus. For children the text should be stringently edited to focus on the main theme in a dramatic, concrete way. The full length drama may exhaust the children's staying power. If an edited text is used, time may allow for some words of homily.

Focusing Experiences

Help the children know the story of the passion, and encourage them to explore and ask questions about it. Placing a cross in a prominent position in the home or classroom will help the children focus on the passion.

Exploring the Word of God

Soldiers guarded Jesus in the Praetorium. He was made to wear the mock robes of a king. It was the custom of the guards to make sport of criminals condemned to die. It added something to the criminal's sentence, another bit of punishment. The soldiers who guarded Jesus, the man from Nazareth who claimed to be king of the Jews, chose him as their king for a laugh, and honored him with mock bows and mock gestures and put a mock robe over his shoulders and a mock crown on his head. It passed the time for them as they waited for the hour of execution and an end to their hours of duty.

I wonder if any of the soldiers saw anything different in Jesus. There might have been one who thought he was different, one with faith who believed in Jesus. Maybe there was one who marched beside him on the way to Calvary and felt honored. Who knows?

Then they led him out to crucify him. On the way they met a man named Simon from Cyrene who was coming into the city from the country. The soldiers forced him to carry Jesus' cross.

That was a strange thing. The strangest thing that ever happened to Simon—being asked to help the man from Nazareth to carry the cross, help the criminal, help the man condemned to die.

Simon sensed Jesus was no criminal. He felt he was in the presence of a man of God. We don't know what came over Simon but we do know that Jesus made such an impression on him that he and his two sons, Alexander and Rufus, became Christians.

The senior army officer present had the rank of centurion. He is remembered for his famous saying: "Truly this man was God's Son!"

It was the duty of the senior officer to see that the sentence of the court was carried out. He ordered the prisoner to be taken under guard to Calvary. There he was crucified according to Roman law. The condemned man died after three hours. The centurion made a report to his authorities giving the time of death and the usual details.

That should have been the end of it, but it is quite clear that the officer kept thinking about the dead man. He came to the conclusion that Jesus was no ordinary criminal, no ordinary man. He was a man of God. God was with him. When Jesus died the officer noticed the strange silence. The world seemed to hush all around to honor this holy man from Nazareth. No wonder the officer said, "Truly this man was God's Son!"

Call to Faith

We are called to celebrate Jesus, who died lovingly and selflessly for us on a cross.

Jesus, you walked along the way to the hill of Calvary for us.

Jesus, you carried the cross for us.

Jesus, even though you stumbled and fell on the way you got to your feet and walked on for us and for our salvation.

Jesus, you suffered the pains of the nails for us.

Jesus, you died for us because you love us beyond all telling.

Call to Action

The passion narrative might take the form of a walk and talk procession around the Way of the Cross in the church.

Encourage families to have a celebration of kissing the cross at home. Make a cross from old wire, nails, and metal. A crucifix made in this way will be full of symbolism for those at home.

Easter Sunday

Gospel
A reading from the holy Gospel according to John (20:1–9)

Early on the first day of the week, while it was still dark, Mary Magdalene came to the tomb and saw that the stone had been removed from the tomb. So she ran and went to Simon Peter and the other disciple, the one whom Jesus loved, and said to them, "They have taken the Lord out of the tomb, and we do not know where they have laid him." Then Peter and the other disciple set out and went toward the tomb. The two were running together, but the other disciple outran Peter and reached the tomb first. He bent down to look in and saw the linen wrappings lying there, but he did not go in. Then Simon Peter came, following him, and went into the tomb. He saw the linen wrappings lying there, and the cloth that had been on Jesus' head, not lying with the linen wrappings but rolled up in a place by itself. Then the other disciple, who reached the tomb first, also went in, and he saw and believed.

The gospel of the Lord.

Overview
The lenten Scriptures led us on this path through the life, mission, and death of Jesus, to the moment of glory when God raised him from the dead to a new life that would be the salvation of many.

The details of the resurrection can be argued about. What happened on Easter Sunday morning is a blur of excitement and surprises. What cannot be argued about, however, is the result of what took place: Witnesses, followers of Jesus, experienced a great surge of faith in God and in the risen Jesus.

Easter Sunday is about faith in the risen Jesus. It is about singing out our joyful alleluias. It is about welcoming our risen Lord. It is about celebrating and celebrating again.

Children will like to savor the Easter story. Your retelling of it will add its own riches.

Focusing Experiences
Do a nature walk before Sunday. Be conscious of life and new growth.

Encourage families at home to talk about the resurrection and the stir it caused in Jerusalem on the fateful Sunday.

Rather than focusing on the details of the empty tomb, help the children focus on the experience the disciples had of the risen Jesus.

Share the sense of the apostles' excitement by decorating the church in an explosion of color.

Exploring the Word of God

Here's the story. Jesus of Nazareth a condemned man, was nailed to a cross on Friday. His body was laid to rest in a tomb. Now, two days later, some women who are his followers go wild with excitement and say he is risen from the dead.

Apparently, Mary Magdalene and some other women went to the tomb early on Sunday morning. They intended to anoint the dead body, wrap it properly in the death clothes, and do what had to be done to give the body a decent burial before the tomb was finally sealed up. The women were surprised to find that the great round stone at the mouth of the tomb had been rolled back. When they peered inside an angel of God stood before them to say that Jesus was risen from the dead and was going to Galilee to meet his followers.

You can believe what you like! Some people said rising from the dead was impossible. They even said it was probably a publicity stunt organized by the friends of Jesus. But the followers of Jesus had it figured all right. They could hardly believe it themselves. God, they said, had raised Jesus from the dead. It was in the air all the time!

"Our master Jesus hinted at a death that would open out into new life." they said. "It's happened now. He is risen from the dead to lead people into new times and new ways with God. The seed that died has now blossomed into new life. There's no mystery about it. The risen Jesus is with us."

Call to Faith

Lord Jesus, you died. You are risen. You are with us.

Lord Jesus, risen from the dead, we praise you. We bless you. We honor you.

Call to Action

Easter time is a time of celebration. Celebrate!

Celebrate this day with Easter alleluias, Easter flowers, an Easter procession, and Easter colors and music to match the joyful mood. This will take advance preparation.

Second Sunday of Easter

Gospel
A reading from the holy Gospel according to John (20:19–31)

When it was evening on that day, the first day of the week, and the doors of the house where the disciples had met were locked for fear of the Jews, Jesus came and stood among them and said, "Peace be with you. As the Father has sent me, so I send you." When he had said this, he breathed on them and said to them, "Receive the Holy Spirit. If you forgive the sins of any, they are forgiven them; if you retain the sins of any, they are retained."

But Thomas (who was called the Twin), one of the twelve, was not with them when Jesus came. So the other disciples told him, "We have seen the Lord." But he said to them, "Unless I see the mark of the nails in his hands, and put my finger in the mark of the nails and my hand in his side, I will not believe."

A week later his disciples were again in the house, and Thomas was with them. Although the doors were shut, Jesus came and stood among them and said, "Peace be with you." Then he said to Thomas, "Put your finger here and see my hands. Reach out your hand and put it in my side. Do not doubt but believe." Thomas answered him, "My Lord and my God!" Jesus said to him, "Have you believed because you have seen me? Blessed are those who have not seen and yet have come to believe."

Now Jesus did many other signs in the presence of his disciples, which are not written in this book. But these are written so that you may come to believe that Jesus is the Messiah, the Son of God, and that through believing you may have life in his name.

The gospel of the Lord.

Overview
The message of today's gospel is about evidence and faith. Hard evidence can only bring us so far in accepting the risen Jesus. There is also a leap into the dark, an acceptance in faith.

The message is embedded in Thomas' story. The children have to tunnel into this story with their imagination (with the help of the homilist or teacher who tunnels with them) to get the groundwork for the message.

From a liturgical point of view, the Easter celebrations continue. The welcome for the risen Jesus goes on apace.

Focusing Experiences

Ask the children to rank in order 1 to 5 the people they give their highest level of belief to: stranger, friend, parent, teacher, priest, hairdresser, shopkeeper, mechanic, park attendant, passer-by, storyteller, lawbreaker, addict.

Ask them why they think some people are more worthy of belief than others.

As an immediate preparation, introduce Thomas, who wanted to believe, but nagging doubt had a stronger hold on him.

Exploring the Word of God

It was tough on Thomas. He was one of them, one of the small band who followed Jesus everywhere. But he wasn't there when the risen Jesus appeared in the room where they were gathered. They tried to share with him the excitement they experienced. They tried to explain their feelings of joy. They told him the story. They gave him the details, every last one. They tried to relive it for him step by step—Jesus dead on the cross, buried in a tomb, had risen from the dead, appeared to them, and spoken with them.

It was no good. He couldn't get into their feelings. He couldn't accept their words. The story stayed cold for him. As far as he was concerned Jesus was still dead. He couldn't bring himself to believe. He couldn't believe in the risen Jesus like they did.

"I didn't see him. I didn't touch him. I don't feel anything," said Thomas. "I cannot believe."

Then Jesus was with them. Just like that! He was right there with them!

"Come near me, Thomas," he said. "Speak to me, touch me."

Belief and amazement were written across Thomas' face. His eyes were full of wonder. His hands were raised to God in gratitude. In a trembling voice he whispered, "My Lord and my God."

The others who saw it were glad for him, were glad for his belief.

Thomas is remembered by the followers of Jesus as the man who doubted. He got the name Doubting Thomas. He did doubt—doubted his friends, doubted himself, doubted that Jesus was risen. But then he believed and he never looked back. He went on his travels for Jesus. He shared his belief in the risen Lord with countless others and held nothing back. He is remembered as a saint.

Call to Faith

We are called to follow the risen Jesus on the evidence of our eyes and ears.

We are called to follow the risen Jesus on the evidence of the disciples.

We are called to follow the risen Jesus on the evidence of our parents, priests, and teachers.

We are called to follow the risen Jesus on the evidence of our hearts.

We are called to have faith in the risen Jesus.

Call to Action

Sing an Easter song to express faith in Jesus.

Take time to underline the "Christ is Risen" headline during the Mass.

Make a public statement (after communion) as a group of Jesus' followers expressing faith in Jesus.

THIRD SUNDAY OF EASTER

Gospel
A reading from the holy Gospel according to Luke (24:35–48)

The disciples told what had happened on the road, and how he had been made known to them in the breaking of the bread.

While they were talking about this, Jesus himself stood among them and said to them, "Peace be with you." They were startled and terrified, and thought that they were seeing a ghost. He said to them, "Why are you frightened, and why do doubts arise in your hearts? Look at my hands and my feet; see that it is I myself. Touch me and see; for a ghost does not have flesh and bones as you see that I have."

And when he had said this, he showed them his hands and his feet. While in their joy they were disbelieving and still wondering, he said to them, "Have you anything here to eat?" They gave him a piece of broiled fish, and he took it and ate in their presence.

The gospel of the Lord.

Overview
The gospel story has a lovely human feel about it. The disciples are scared. They think the risen Jesus is a ghost. It is only when he asks for something to eat that they relax and welcome him. This story from Luke serves to underline the reality and the presence of Jesus risen-from-the-dead.

The homilist will need to feel his or her way into this story, giving it twists and turns like Luke does, to capture the humanity and the reality of the risen Jesus for the children.

Focusing Experiences
Remember those television programs where members of a family who haven't seen each other for years and years and are separated by thousands of miles of land and sea, suddenly meet in the studio and it's a total surprise? Think of their shock, excitement, and disbelief. Imagine the disciples talking of their own experience.

Exploring the Word of God

We were together in the room talking about the latest news that came as it happens from the town of Emmaus. Two of our people met a stranger on the way to that town. The stranger turned out to be the risen Jesus. That was a shock for them, a total surprise—completely unexpected.

The two of them came back right away to Jerusalem to share their news with us even though it was the middle of the night. We were all agog with the good news they had about meeting Jesus. We were going over it and wondering what it all meant when, suddenly, Jesus was there with us, right there with us.

We just froze. He spoke to us. He said, "Peace be with you."

It was his voice all right. Not a bit of difference. But when you've just buried someone it is hard to face them in real life again. We couldn't take it in. We said nothing to him. We just stared.

We all hear stories about the dead coming back to haunt the living and things like that. And here was someone coming back to us from the dead. I, for one, thought maybe it was my turn to leave the living and join the dead. I was frightened.

"It's me," he said, "don't be frightened, "It's really me. Don't doubt it. Are these scars real? On my hands? On my feet? Look me in the eye. It's me."

We were nervous. There were plenty of white faces and scared looks around.

To put us at our ease, he said, "Have you anything to eat? I'm hungry."

We had just grilled a bit of whitefish. We offered him a piece and he sat with us and ate it. Then we all relaxed. We knew it was him, and we made him welcome.

Jesus is risen from the dead—that's for sure. But it's only the beginning. There's more to come. We have plans to change the world. We'll tell you about it later!

Call to Faith

Jesus, you are risen and with us.
> You are with us now.
> At Mass we share a meal with you now as friends should.
> We are enjoying your friendship.
> You mean a lot to us.
> We want you to be part of our lives today and always.

Call to Action

Jesus shared a meal with the two friends at Emmaus. In the gospel story he shares a meal with his disciples. At Mass we share a meal with the risen Jesus. This is an opportunity to emphasize the meal aspect of the Mass in the actions, in the songs, in the prayers, in the words, and in the commentary and introductions we use.

In their family meals at home invite the parents to pay a small tribute to our friend Jesus. Encourage families to talk about how what they do at home—gathered for a meal—is linked to the great Mass meal where Jesus is present among us in a most wonderful and special way.

Fourth Sunday of Easter

Gospel
A reading from the holy Gospel according to John (10:11–18)

Jesus said, "I am the good shepherd. The good shepherd lays down his life for the sheep. The hired hand, who is not the shepherd and does not own the sheep, sees the wolf coming and leaves the sheep and runs away—and the wolf snatches them and scatters them. The hired hand runs away because a hired hand does not care for the sheep. I am the good shepherd. I know my own and my own know me, just as the Father knows me and I know the Father. And I lay down my life for the sheep. I have other sheep that do not belong to this fold. I must bring them also, and they will listen to my voice. So there will be one flock, one shepherd. For this reason the Father loves me, because I lay down my life in order to take it up again. No one takes it from me, but I lay it down of my own accord. I have power to lay it down, and I have power to take it up again. I have received this command from my Father."

The gospel of the Lord.

Overview
This gospel reading both praises Jesus and tells us more of who he is for us.

It is a proclamation of the risen Jesus as shepherd.

In our preaching and teaching we need to explore the imagery of shepherd with the children and follow this with a prayer to Jesus the Shepherd. To understand that Jesus is shepherd is a beginning. To express it in prayer is faith in action.

This is also World Day of Prayer for Vocations.

Focusing Experiences
Shepherd is synonymous with care, concern, dedication, and love. We may know a gardener who loves his or her plants and who might even talk to them. We may know a nature lover who defends trees and green spaces and is dedicated to conservation in a serious way. We may have a friend who loves cats or dogs in a way that is very special.

We want the children to understand the richness of meaning and experience that the word "shepherd" evokes. Because the biblical shepherd is not a part of our culture we have to use other images to communicate the friendship, love, closeness, and intimacy that the biblical word "shepherd" conveys.

Exploring the Word of God

When I hear the word shepherd I think of mountains and sheep. I hear the voice of the shepherd echoing in the hills. I hear the commands to his dog. I see the dog moving ever so gently alongside the sheep, at one moment gliding along the ground, then breaking into a mad dash to keep the sheep in formation. The shepherd is like a king among the sheep, lord of the mountain, lord of the sheep.

Shepherd is a very old word to describe a very old job going back to the time when humanity itself was young. The word shepherd is mentioned in the Bible, and many of the famous people in the Bible were shepherds. There was one thing that everyone knew about a shepherd—the sheep were his number one priority. The sheep were as precious to him as life itself. They were precious because he knew them all and loved them all. Many a shepherd in Bible days died defending his sheep against wolves or robbers. Stories were told of shepherds who climbed down cliffs at the risk of their lives in fierce gales to rescue sheep hanging on ledges, or of shepherds who trekked for days and nights into lonely places to find one lost sheep.

Shepherds were simply great people. They were out on their own, a class apart. They were there when they were needed. That was the greatest tribute of all.

Priests are sometimes called shepherds of their people. They are greatly honored by this title.

God was called a Shepherd. People thought this was a fitting title for God, who loved the people and cared for them.

Jesus is called Shepherd. He even said that to the people: "Let me be your shepherd. I would be honored to serve you as Shepherd."

Call to Faith

Lord Jesus you are the Shepherd who loves us.
    Be near us in the early morning when the day dawns.
    Be near us when the sun is shining in our lives.
    Be near us in times of joy, of laughter, of games.
    Be near us at home, at school, or wherever we are.
    Lord Jesus, you are the Shepherd who cares for us.

Be near us when night falls and darkness closes in around us.
Be near us when we are lonely.
Be near us when we are sad.
Be near us when we feel hurt or let down or misunderstood.
Be near us when friends are absent.
Be near us when times are tough at school or at home.
Lord Jesus, we call you Shepherd.
Be near today and always, forever and ever. Amen.

Call to Action

Sing or listen to a solo rendering of Psalm 23: "The Lord is my Shepherd."

During the various parts of the Mass use the title Shepherd as often as possible when you refer to the risen Jesus.

On this Vocations Sunday give a prominent role to young people in the parish who are serving God's community in a special way.

In class or at home, ask the children to draw a dramatic scene depicting a shepherd in a dangerous situation defending or rescuing a lost sheep.

Fifth Sunday of Easter

Gospel
A reading from the holy Gospel according to John (15:1–8)

Jesus said, "I am the true vine, and my Father is the vine-grower. He removes every branch in me that bears no fruit. Every branch that bears fruit he prunes to make it bear more fruit. You have already been cleansed by the word that I have spoken to you. Abide in me as I abide in you. Just as the branch cannot bear fruit by itself unless it abides in the vine, neither can you unless you abide in me. I am the vine, you are the branches. Those who abide in me and I in them bear much fruit, because apart from me you can do nothing. Whoever does not abide in me is thrown away like a branch and withers; such branches are gathered, thrown into the fire, and burned. If you abide in me, and my words abide in you, ask for whatever you wish, and it will be done for you."

The gospel of the Lord.

Overview
On this Sunday we are treated to one of John's reflections, one of his meditations on the relationship between Jesus and his followers. It is a relationship that can be either vital, living, and fresh, or hollow and dead. The imagery is drawn from the world of vine trees and grape cultivation.

We should not be afraid to let the homily for children take the form of a short meditation on our relationship with Jesus using the imagery of the gospel, but the atmosphere has to be right. It might be a good idea to ask the children to close their eyes as we lead them into the imagery. If one can focus on a real tree (through the window of the classroom or church) or gather around a real tree on the church grounds, so much the better.

Focusing Experiences
Parents, children, go outside! Look at trees, look at branches that grow so marvelously out of the tree. The tree is a great living thing. Look at the deadwood hanging from the tree or already rotting on the ground.

Jesus used the image of trees and living branches to explain great truths about himself and God. The tree that people noticed most in his day was the vine. Every garden had some.

The vine is a small tree, like a shrub. It grows about waist high. It has a sort of wizened, twisted trunk. The branches are about the length of your arm and seem to come straight out from the trunk. Bunches of grapes grow on the branches. The grapes are collected and pressed to make wine.

Vine trees need plenty of care if they are to produce good quality grapes.

Exploring the Word of God

Jesus says, "I am the vine and you, who are my followers, are the branches. The branches grow out of the vine. One tree. One life. One flow. You and I are one. We cannot be separated. We are meant to be together.

"Watch the workers in the vineyard. They cut away dead branches. They prune away wood that will never produce grapes. They hack and chop and cut.

"Some followers of mine are dead branches. There is no life in them, no growth, no fruit. Some of my followers have no life and no love in them. They don't want to walk with me. They have turned their back on my Father's love. They can't be allowed to hang on, to suck the life and the goodness out of the others. The whole tree would rot. They have to go. They have to be separated. It's the only way.

"The vine and the branches are one piece, one movement, one growth out of the ground and into the sky. You are my fruitful followers. We grow together. We are one in friendship. We are one in love. We are one in what we are doing for God.

"Together we will change the world. We have the heart for it. We have the energy for it. We have the love to change the world because the love flows in us and around us. It is part of what we are."

Call to Faith

You are the vine. We are the branches that live in you.

We share your strength.

We share your energy.

We share your love.

We are called to love like Jesus, to make good things happen for our friends, to share.

Call to Action

At various parts of the Mass this week, use the imagery from the gospel story to focus on a healthy and living relationship with the risen Jesus.

Arrange a penitential service for later in the week using the imagery of trees and branches, growth, life, and vitality to represent our thriving relationship with Jesus. Use rotten or dead wood to focus on our faults, our negative attitudes, and the down side of our relationship with Jesus.

Sixth Sunday of Easter

Gospel
A reading from the holy Gospel according to John (15:9–17)

Jesus said to his disciples, "As the Father has loved me, so I have loved you; abide in my love. If you keep my commandments, you will abide in my love, just as I have kept my Father's commandments and abide in his love. I have said these things to you so that my joy may be in you, and that your joy may be complete.

"This is my commandment, that you love one another as I have loved you. No one has greater love than this, to lay down one's life for one's friends. You are my friends if you do what I command you. I am giving you these commands so that you may love one another."

The gospel of the Lord.

Overview
Love is what God the Father gave to Jesus. Love is what Jesus gives to us. Love is what we who are followers of the risen Jesus must give to one another.

The entreaty of today's gospel is challenging and direct—"Love one another."

We should try to help the children understand that the love they experience at home and everywhere around them is a manifestation, an echo, a glimpse, a reflection of God's love.

Focusing Experiences
God's love is all around us, touching us. God's love is alive in our world.

It is in the singing of the birds down in a meadow. It is in the sparkling stream that runs through a field. It is in the magnificent setting sun that goes down behind the mountains. It is in the bloom of gardens. It is in the color of the fields by the creek. It is in the little flower that lives in the crevice of a rock high in the hills. It is in the shining waters of a lake.

It is especially alive in the people around us, our neighbors, our friends, our family. All around us God's love comes alive to please us and comfort us and give us joy.

God's love is in our city, in the colors we see on billboards, on neon lights, in shops and shopping malls, in the noises we hear, in the shapes of the buildings we look at, in the skyline that encircles us, in the traffic that weaves and dances past us, and in the music that is played around us. Above all, God's love comes to us in the people who are part of our lives.

(The immediate challenge for the homilist will be to give expression to God's love as it is echoed in the local neighborhood and in the community that gathers around the altar.)

Exploring the Word of God

God's love comes to us in a special way through Jesus. He shows us how to love one another.

He touched the leper with love and gave him a feeling of belonging. He touched the sick little girl with love and gave her back to her parents.

He touches us with love. He speaks with love.

He forgives with love.

Love is the legacy Jesus gave us. Love is the inheritance he entrusted to us. Love is what he asks us to spread around.

Call to Faith

"Love one another" is the motto he wants us all to live by.

Love is the slogan he wants us to remember.

Love is the calling he wants us to follow.

Love is the feeling he wants us to experience.

Love is the kind word he wants us to say.

Love is the helpful action he wants us to do at home when tired parents need our help.

Love is the smile he wants us to give willingly when smiles are in short supply.

Love is the harmony he wants us to create when harmony is about to lose out to hot tempers.

Love is everything good he wants us to do when it would quite easy to do nothing.

Love is his way. He wants it to be our way too.

Call to Action

Opportunities should be taken to focus on God's love, Jesus' love, and on our call to love one another.

The community could express its love for the children today in a tangible way; for example, with a party in the community center.

This might be a time to launch a significant community project.

ASCENSION

Gospel
A reading from the holy Gospel according to Mark (16:15–20)

Jesus appeared to the eleven themselves as they were sitting at the table; and he upbraided them for their lack of faith and stubbornness, because they had not believed those who saw him after he had risen. And he said to them, "Go into all the world and proclaim the good news to the whole creation. The one who believes and is baptized will be saved; but the one who does not believe will be condemned. And these signs will accompany those who believe: by using my name they will cast out demons; they will speak in new tongues; they will pick up snakes in their hands, and if they drink any deadly thing, it will not hurt them; they will lay their hands on the sick, and they will recover."

So then the Lord Jesus, after he had spoken to them, was taken up into heaven and sat down at the right hand of God. And they went out and proclaimed the good news everywhere, while the Lord worked with them and confirmed the message by the signs that accompanied it.

The gospel of the Lord.

Overview
The apostles are sent out on their mission. Jesus takes his place with the Father in glory. The work of Jesus goes on everywhere.

The Ascension concept is difficult. It is very theological. It is about a new role for Jesus at the right hand of the Father and a new role for the disciples among the people. Rather than focus on the physical aspects of the Ascension, we should explore the challenge implicit in Jesus' movement into new relationships.

It is worth telling today's gospel story in radio script form (from *The Columba Lectionary for Masses with Children*). Involve parents in the various speaking parts.

Focusing Experiences
Help the children think about:
    meeting the challenge of getting to know new friends

meeting the challenge of getting used to a new school
having the experience of meeting new people on vacation
facing new challenges in sports
facing new responsibilities as we grow older
new beginnings when things go wrong for us.

Exploring the Word of God

The risen Jesus is with the disciples, but in a new way. It's time for new beginnings.

Voice 1 I have no heart. I'm fed up and depressed. It's the end.

Voice 2 Jesus is not with us. He's gone from us.

Voice 3 All the great hopes we had—a new kingdom, changing the world, bringing people back to God.

Voice 1 It sounded great when he was with us. Remember the people flocking to hear him? Remember how we had to hold the crowds back? Remember how sinners changed their ways and came to him to be brought back into God's friendship?

Voice 2 And the sick who flocked to him. And the lepers. Remember the leper he touched who went away healed, praising God?

Voice 3 It looked like the beginning of something great. I would have gone to the ends of the earth with him.

Voice 1 I would have died for him.

Voice 2 He died on the cross for us. He never gave in. He died praising God. What a terrible loss.

Voice 3 He was God's chosen one. It's not the end. It cannot be the end. I believe that what he started will not come to a sudden end.

Narrator Then the risen Jesus stood among them and they were greatly surprised. He put a new heart into them and a new confidence.

Jesus No more sadness. No more waiting. Make a beginning. Spread the word of God. Go out to the ends of the earth. Have no fear. I will be with you. Our work is just beginning. (silence)

Jesus Build a new world in my name. Put things right. Oppose evil. Never give in. (silence)

Jesus Give people hope. Work for a better world. For a new world. (silence)

Jesus Spread the kingdom of God. I will be with you. (silence)

Narrator They went out with a new confidence and spoke their message everywhere about a new world. The Lord Jesus worked with them, and their work for the kingdom of God prospered.

Call to Faith

We are called to be followers of Jesus.

We are called to do a job for God.

We are called to continue the work of Jesus.

We are called to make our home a place of harmony and love.

We are called to make our school a place of friendship, fun, under-standing, and fair play.

We are called to be generous with money. We are called to think of others when we have money.

We are called to be generous with our time. We are called to think of how we might help family and friends in our spare time.

We are called to be generous with praise. We are called to give praise and encouragement to friends.

We are called to follow Jesus in what we say and do.

Call to Action

Involve parents in the radio script.

Sing songs of mission.

Take on a mission enterprise. Through a mission organization make links with children in other lands. Write to them.

Have a collection of clothes or donations for a worthy mission cause.

Seventh Sunday of Easter

Gospel
A reading from the holy Gospel according to John (17:11–19)

Jesus looked up to heaven and said, "Holy Father, protect them in your name that you have given me, so that they may be one, as we are one. While I was with them I protected them in your name that you have given me. I guarded them, and not one of them was lost except the one destined to be lost, so that the scripture might be fulfilled.

"I have given them your word, and the world has hated them. I am not asking you to take them out of the world, but I ask you to protect them from the evil one. Sanctify them in the truth; your word is truth. As you have sent me into the world, so I have sent them into the world. And for their sakes I sanctify myself, so that they also may be sanctified in truth."

The gospel of the Lord.

Overview
Today, Jesus prays a prayer of blessing over his disciples and urges them to carry on his mission.

This is a blessing too, for the domestic church, the family in the home. Jesus' mission is entrusted to them, too.

The homily might have as its high point the priest's blessing of parents and the parents' blessing of children. This will give a practical expression to Jesus' blessing and his call to action.

Focusing Experiences
A blessing is an important thing.

Children of every generation put a high value on their parents' blessing. It might be a few words like "God bless you" before they settle down for the night, or a stroke on the cheek as the child falls asleep, or a pat on the back, or a hug of endearment. It might be a wave of the hand as they go from home or a little memento packed into a bag to remind children of parents' love. The words, the wave, the hugs, the kisses are signs of love, signs of parents' affection for their children, signs of parents' blessing. A blessing is a gift from parents. It is a kind of protection that parents wish on their children. They want their love to go with the children. A blessing is a wish that goodness will surround, accompany, and follow the one who is blessed.

People sometimes go to the priest for a blessing. They ask the priest to pray that God's love will come on them, especially if they are facing some difficult endeavor.

Babies are blessed in baptism by their parents as a loving welcome into God's family.

Children are blessed with holy oil in confirmation for the task they are undertaking for God.

People go on pilgrimage to holy places for the blessing they will receive.

On Easter Sunday the Pope gives his blessing to the world.

At Mass the priest blesses the people.

We bless ourselves with holy water.

Exploring the Word of God
Jesus said a prayer of blessing over his disciples:
May the blessing of God be on them.
Keep them safe when they are in danger.
Guide them in the way of love.
Support them in danger or hardship.
Give them heart when they are feeling low.
Comfort them when they are lonely.
Lift them up when they are weak.
Bring them home when they are lost.
Keep them in your care always.

Call to Faith
We are all disciples.
We need the blessing of Jesus.
We are called to receive the blessing of Jesus.

Call to Action
A Blessing on Parents
(As part of the homily the priest blesses the parents)
The blessing of Jesus on you for all that you are doing for your children.
A blessing on you to be wise and strong and loving.
May your words be full of kindness,
and your actions full of compassion.
And when you are short tempered,
May your children understand that they are loved through it all.
May you and your children grow together in faith and hope and love.

A Blessing on Children
(The parents bless the children, laying hands on the child's head.)

God's blessing on you, to give you strength.
God's blessing on you to give you faith in Jesus.
God's blessing on you to give you love.

PENTECOST SUNDAY

First Reading
A reading from the Acts of the Apostles (2:1–11)

When the day of Pentecost had come, they were all together in one place. And suddenly from heaven there came a sound like the rush of a violent wind, and it filled the entire house where they were sitting. Divided tongues, as of fire, appeared among them, and a tongue rested on each of them. All of them were filled with the Holy Spirit and began to speak in other languages, as the Spirit gave them ability.

Now there were devout Jews from every nation under heaven living in Jerusalem. And at this sound the crowd gathered and was bewildered, because each one heard them speaking in the native language of each. Amazed and astonished they asked, "Are not all of these who are speaking Galileans? And how is it that we hear, each of us, in our own native language? In our own languages we hear them speaking about God's deeds of power."

The word of the Lord.

Overview
This Sunday would seem incomplete without the Pentecost story (the first reading) at the heart of the homily. It is a story of action and energy. The Spirit gets things moving.

It's a time for energy in the community at the service of the risen Jesus.

The homily for the children will have its own high point in the action elements that accompany it.

Focusing Experiences
What do you know about enthusiasm? Ever seen it? Experienced it?

What do you know about energy and enthusiasm put to work?

What projects did you undertake with great enthusiasm, with great energy?

What influences people to get involved in projects?

What influences you to get involved in your projects?

Exploring the Word of God

The disciples were feeling a bit down. They wanted to go on doing Jesus' work but they had no heart for it. They were together in a room, huddled round a fire. They tried to convince themselves they were planning for the future, but they were really feeling afraid. In a way they were trying to talk themselves out of a job they couldn't face.

"We have no education," they said. "How can we spread the name of Jesus? We have no practice in speech making. We'll be swallowed up in the sneers and laughter. How can we face arguments from scholars and experts? We'll be a laughing stock. There are a lot of people out there who don't want the name of Jesus spread around. They'll use words to confuse and embarrass us. They'll play tricks on us with their fine-sounding phrases. They want his memory to die. They won't have much trouble with us. Whether we go or stay his name and his memory are going to die anyway."

Someone else tried to sound cheerful: "But he said he would send the Spirit to help us."

But their gloomy faces told their own story. They didn't really feel anything could be done for them.

Then in a flash the Holy Spirit of God was over them. The Spirit of God got into their blood, into their bones, into their heads, into their hearts. They felt themselves lifted up, renewed, refreshed, energized. They felt different. They felt confidence. They felt ready to take on the world. They rushed out of the room and down into the street to make their first speeches about Jesus. It was an amazing turnaround. Unbelievable!

They and their friends and those followers of Christ who came after them have been moving around at a hectic pace ever since. They've reached out into Europe, the Americas, Africa, India, Asia, Australia.

It was the Holy Spirit that made the difference.

Call to Faith

Come, Holy Spirit, fill the hearts of your faithful people.
Send us out with a song of joy.
Send us out with a dream to make things different.
Send us out with Jesus in our minds, on our lips, and in our hearts.
Send us out to make things happen.
Fill us with energy and enthusiasm for the work of the risen Jesus.

Call to Action

Sing songs of the Holy Spirit.
Listen to some verses from the Alleluia Chorus—there are plenty of recordings around.

At Mass, extend the final *Go forth in Peace* to include a call to live Spirit-filled lives.

Ask someone engaged in a Christian endeavor to say a word about their ministry.

It might be a good time to renew confirmation undertakings.

Is there something needs doing in the community that requires energy and enthusiasm that the children could be involved in? Consider getting involved.

Gospel
A reading from the holy Gospel according to John (20:19–23)

When it was evening on that day, the first day of the week, and the doors of the house where the disciples had met were locked for fear of the Jews, Jesus came and stood among them and said, "Peace be with you. As the Father has sent me, so I send you."When he had said this, he breathed on them and said to them, "Receive the Holy Spirit. If you forgive the sins of any, they are forgiven them; if you retain the sins of any, they are retained."

The gospel of the Lord.

TRINITY SUNDAY

Gospel
A reading from the holy Gospel according to Matthew (28:16–20)

Now the eleven disciples went to Galilee, to the mountain to which Jesus had directed them. When they saw him, they worshiped him; but some doubted. And Jesus came and said to them, "All authority in heaven and on earth has been given to me. Go therefore and make disciples of all nations, baptizing them in the name of the Father and of the Son and of the Holy Spirit, and teaching them to obey everything that I have commanded you. And remember, I am with you always, to the end of the age."

The gospel of the Lord.

Overview
We are baptized in the name of the Father and of the Son and of the Holy Spirit. We are confirmed in their name. We are married in their name. We are anointed in their name. We are buried in their name. We bless ourselves at the beginning and at the end of each day. All these very significant actions are done in the name of the Father, and of the Son, and of the Holy Spirit. The Father, Son, and Holy Spirit must be at the heart of what we believe to be important about our Faith. The disciples are sent out on their mission and told that they are to dedicate themselves to baptizing people in the name of the Father and of the Son and of the Holy Spirit.

We have to give the children a sense of the authority and the dignity of these names. And we have to offer a meaning to explain the richness embedded in this age-old trinitarian formula.

Focusing Experiences
Discuss with the children the practice of invoking the names of great institutions of state when matters of importance are at stake.

In the name of the law I ask you...

In the name of the state I summon you...

In the name of the president I sign this declaration...

In the name of the Court I find the defendant not guilty...

Names can be important. Sometimes we invoke a great name as a sign that the action being undertaken is for the good of the whole community. It is a clear signal that the good of the community is involved, and the name is invoked to give strength to what is being said or done. The action has the highest backing. The action has the weight, strength, and authority of the whole community behind it. We do not claim to have the authority ourselves. We invoke the authority. We invoke the name.

Only some specially chosen people are entitled to invoke the names of great institutions—people who can be trusted, people who will not abuse the privilege.

Exploring the Word of God

The disciples are sent out to baptize in the name of the Father and in the name of the Son and in the name of the Holy Spirit.

In the name of the Father...

The Father is everything that we can imagine about the wonder and the power and the beauty and effect of love. The Father is love.

In the name of the Son, Jesus...

Jesus is our friend. Jesus is the voice of God. Jesus is the love of God among us. Jesus is the power of God inviting us into God's friendship.

In the name of the Holy Spirit...

The Spirit inspires us to do deeds of goodness, to act like Jesus, to walk in the footsteps of Jesus.

It is our belief that a triangle of love exists between Father, Son, and Holy Spirit. When we talk about God in all glory, in all majesty, in all wonder, we are talking about a triangle of love that is alive and reaching out to us and taking us into its core. We are talking of Father, Son, and Spirit, bound together in a circle of love that is pulsing with life. When we call on the name of the Trinity we invoke God in all wonder, in all holiness, in all love. We have said everything about God when we call on the Trinity to bless our actions.

Call to Faith

In the name of the Father and of the Son and of the Holy Spirit:
    We ask the blessing of God.
    We ask for love.
    We ask for forgiveness.
    We ask for inspiration.
    We ask for peace.
    We ask for a new world.
    In the name of the Father and of the Son and of the Holy Spirit:
    We ask for work for our unemployed.
    We ask for refuge for our refugees.
    We ask for food for those in famine areas.

We ask for justice for those denied justice.

We ask for compassion for those who have sinned against the community.

In the name of the Father and of the Son and of the Holy Spirit:

We ask for the love of Jesus to touch us in all that we do and in all that we say today and always, forever and ever.

Call to Action

Sing a hymn to the Trinity.

Each time the name of the Trinity is invoked in this Mass it should be highlighted by a silence, or by an introductory focusing statement or phrase.

Extend the final blessing to include the following:

"May the blessing of Almighty God who is our Father, Mother, Shepherd; and the Son Jesus who is our Friend, Leader, Savior; and the Holy Spirit who inspires us to good action; be upon us now and always, for ever and ever."

THE BODY AND BLOOD OF CHRIST

Gospel
A reading from the holy Gospel according to Mark (14:12–16, 22–26)

On the first day of Unleavened Bread, when the Passover lamb is sacrificed, his disciples said to him, "Where do you want us to go and make the preparations for you to eat the Passover?" So he sent two of his disciples, saying to them, "Go into the city, and a man carrying a jar of water will meet you; follow him, and wherever he enters, say to the owner of the house, 'The Teacher asks, Where is my guest room where I may eat the Passover with my disciples?' He will show you a large room upstairs, furnished and ready. Make preparations for us there." So the disciples set out and went to the city, and found everything as he had told them; and they prepared the Passover meal.

While they were eating, he took a loaf of bread and after blessing it he broke it, gave it to them, and said, "Take; this is my body." Then he took a cup, and after giving thanks he gave it to them, and all of them drank from it. He said to them, "This is my blood of the covenant, which is poured out for many. Truly I tell you, I will never again drink of the fruit of the vine until the day when I drink it new in the kingdom of God."

The gospel of the Lord.

Overview
This gospel reading has deep links into Old Testament ritual and theology. The Old Testament understanding and experience of sacrifice and covenant is being renewed. A new order in our relationship with God is emerging. Jesus offers a new sacrifice. Jesus establishes a new covenant.

We celebrate our feast of *Corpus Christi* by establishing links for the children between the Passover meal and the cross of Calvary, between Mass and the sacrifice of Jesus.

Later we celebrate the sacramental presence of Jesus with a *Corpus Christi* procession. We express our belief with our feet and with our voices.

Focusing Experiences

Place the cross in a prominent place at home or school. Help the children understand that at Mass the sacrifice of Jesus is replayed, re-enacted, lived out again. Jesus gives himself to the Father at Mass with all the love he gave on the cross. It is the sacrifice of love offered again by Jesus.

Exploring the Word of God

Jesus instructed the disciples to go into the city to a certain place where they would meet a man carrying a bucket of water. They were to follow him wherever he led them. The man with the bucket of water led them to a house where they were asked their business by the owner. They were instructed by Jesus to say, "Show us the room for the Passover meal Jesus is to have with his disciples." When they said this they were shown a room where a table was laid for the Passover meal. They prepared food for the table and got everything ready.

Some time later Jesus and the other disciples joined them. As was the custom, Jesus sat at the head of the table and the disciples sat round him. All of them had celebrated the Passover meal year after year since childhood. They did what was always done at the Passover meal. But something else was done—something new. They remembered very clearly that Jesus took bread and broke it and said, "This is my body," and shared the broken bread with them, a piece to each one. That was different. That was a shock. That had not happened before for them. It made them wonder. Later on when Jesus died on the cross it became clear what he meant. His body was broken on the cross for them, given and shared with great love. The bread was broken for them. It was the story of his life. The bread broken was his body broken. The sacrifice of his body with love. Jesus gave his life as a sacrifice of love.

At the Passover meal he took the chalice of wine and said, "This is my blood" and he gave them the chalice and they all sipped from it. Later on when he died they knew what he meant. His life's blood was given for them on the cross. His sacrifice in love was offered for all people.

After the Holy Spirit came on the first Christians they began to meet to have a Passover meal like Jesus had. The first Christians felt that Jesus was with them with all the love he showed for them on the cross. It was his sacrifice of love again, repeated. It was a wonderful feeling to have Jesus present with the community in that way.

And the followers of Jesus have continued to do this down through the ages to today. The priest says the words of Jesus over the bread: "This is my body." He also said the words of Jesus over the wine: "This is my blood."

Call to Faith

Jesus, you died for us on the cross.

You offered a sacrifice of love for us.

At this Mass you offer your sacrifice of love again.

We are here with you to witness this event.

We are here to be part of that offering.

We are here to join in that offering of love.

We are here to add our love to your great offering.

The bread we eat in communion is broken and shared among us.

Your body was broken in death and became a gift of love that is shared by all.

We eat the bread that was broken.

We share in your life.

We share in your love.

Call to Action

Highlight the Mass as sacrifice and as offering by appropriate songs and commentary.

The word "offer" and the word "sacrifice" should be incorporated as often as possible in introductions, commentary, and prayers at this Mass.

A special prayer offering our love to God should be included.

Celebrate with a *Corpus Christi* procession.

SECOND SUNDAY IN ORDINARY TIME

Gospel
A reading from the holy Gospel according to John (1:35–42)

The next day John again was standing with two of his disciples, and as he watched Jesus walk by, he exclaimed, "Look, here is the Lamb of God!" The two disciples heard him say this, and they followed Jesus. When Jesus turned and saw them following, he said to them, "What are you looking for?" They said to him, "Rabbi" (which translated means Teacher), "where are you staying?" He said to them, "Come and see." They came and saw where he was staying, and they remained with him that day. It was about four o'clock in the afternoon. One of the two who heard John speak and followed him was Andrew, Simon Peter's brother. He first found his brother Simon and said to him, "We have found the Messiah" (which is translated Anointed). He brought Simon to Jesus, who looked at him and said, "You are Simon son of John. You are to be called Cephas" (which is translated Peter).

The gospel of the Lord.

Overview
John the Baptist's role is to share Jesus with the world. In today's reading we hear the story of John "sharing" Jesus with his band of disciples. Andrew, who was one of those disciples, goes on to "share" Jesus with his brother Simon.

"Sharing" Jesus is at the heart of discipleship.

Focusing Experiences
Help the children to appreciate the notion of sharing as a way of helping others to appreciate something we think is important. For example: introducing a toy to others to make that toy more loved, more appreciated; introducing a game to others to help them to see the worth we put on it; sharing news because the news will help our friends to understand something that we think they should understand; sharing friends to allow others to appreciate these friends whom we think are worth appreciating.

Exploring the Word of God

John the Baptist was a leader, a prophet, a rabbi. His disciples gathered around him to hear his words, to learn from his wisdom, to become masters one day like him.

John the Baptist was a man of God. He understood God's ways. He recognized Jesus as God's Messiah. He said to his disciples: "That is God's Messiah!" He wanted to share the Messiah with those who were closest to him. Andrew and another disciple left John and sought out Jesus. They stayed with Jesus three days. After that they wanted to become disciples of Jesus. John the Baptist didn't mind them leaving him. He was glad to "share" Jesus with them.

After being with Jesus, Andrew went home to his own place and spoke to his brother Simon. "We have found the Messiah," he said. When Simon heard this he wanted to become a disciple of Jesus. Andrew and Simon became followers of Jesus and went everywhere with him.

Call to Faith

We honor those who have shared Jesus with us.

We honor our parents who shared Jesus with us on the day we were baptized, on that very day when they signed the cross of Jesus on our foreheads.

We thank our parents who share Jesus with us in many ways as we grow up, especially in the way they want us to relate to God and to our family and friends.

We honor and thank our teachers who share Jesus with us in stories, songs, and discussions.

We honor and thank our priest who shares Jesus with us at Mass and helps us to meet Jesus in other sacraments.

We honor and thank all our friends who share Jesus with us by the way they talk and act and live.

Call to Action

Invite a teacher to give a two-minute testimony on the songs, drawings, activities, and discussions that represent how he or she is sharing Jesus with the children.

Provide an opportunity for the children themselves to thank parents, teachers, priests, and others for "sharing" Jesus with them.

This might be a good occasion for parents to review their faith input at home. This review could be facilitated by other parents, priests, and teachers.

THIRD SUNDAY IN ORDINARY TIME

Gospel
A reading from the holy Gospel according to Mark (1:14–20)

As Jesus passed along the Sea of Galilee, he saw Simon and his brother Andrew casting a net into the sea—for they were fishermen. And Jesus said to them, "Follow me and I will make you fish for people." And immediately they left their nets and followed him. As he went a little farther, he saw James son of Zebedee and his brother John, who were in their boat mending the nets. Immediately he called them; and they left their father Zebedee in the boat with the hired men, and followed him.

The gospel of the Lord.

Overview
People at that time had an intense interest in the Messiah. Everybody was on the lookout for the Messiah. It was in people's blood, in their consciousness, in their memory, in their upbringing. News of the Messiah grabbed headlines in people's talk all the time.

James and John felt themselves called to follow Jesus. They were sons of Zebedee. Their father, naturally, was a bit taken aback when they left to follow Jesus. There was fishing to be done and a catch to be sold. But he understood these things to do with the Messiah. They wanted to serve. They were cut out for it and happy doing it. And he wasn't going to stand in their way.

They recognized Jesus as the Messiah. They heard his call. They left their boats and gear and followed him. It was as simple and direct as that. James and John became disciples of Jesus.

Focusing Experiences
Explore the idea of "following."
> We follow trends in clothes.
> We follow pop stars and personalities.
> We follow trends in music.
> We have portraits of "stars" pinned up on our walls.
> Some people follow poets or writers and get inspiration from them.
> Some people follow a great movement to save our planet or to free the environment from pollution.

Others follow a calling to promote peace or human rights or civil liberties.

Other follow and support campaigns to spread justice.

Others follow a calling to save animals from cruelty.

Adults follow political leaders and are inspired by them.

We all have people in our lives to whom we look for inspiration and leadership and a cause worth supporting.

The disciples were following their particular cause. Their interest was in God, God's people, and God's world. They were convinced Jesus was the one who would show them the way to find God. They looked to Jesus for inspiration. They were ready to build a new world with him.

Exploring the Word of God

(Exploring the Word of God this week might take the form of a radio play between an interviewer and the father of James and John.)

Interviewer	Zebedee, you're the father of James and John. They left you to follow Jesus.
Zebedee	They left me to follow a good man. I have no regrets.
Interviewer	Their leaving must have been a bit sudden for you.
Zebedee	It was a bit sudden. My two sons and I were doing well in the fishing business. Good catches, good money. And then they were gone, following Jesus as his disciples.
Interviewer	How are you managing now?
Zebedee	I depend on the hired men. They're not the same as sons, but I get by.
Interviewer	Do your sons know what they've let themselves in for? Preaching must be very different from fishing!
Zebedee	I've heard Jesus preaching. He doesn't mince his words. He tells people to change their evil ways and repent. And let me tell you, there is plenty of evil around. Jesus is bringing the people back to God. The work my boys are doing with Jesus is the work of prophets and priests. I'm proud of them for it.
Interviewer	Ah, but will the people listen to them?
Zebedee	They listened to the prophet Jonah in the old days, didn't they, when he went to Nineveh? Jesus and my sons will have to take their chances. God will be with them. Their work is God's work, and it will prosper.

Call to Faith

We are called to follow Jesus.
  We are called to love.
  We are called to share.

We are called to be generous.

We are called to walk in the new way with Jesus.

We are called to build a new world at home, at school, wherever we are.

We are called to make Jesus the inspiration of our lives.

We are called to be, in our own way, disciples of Jesus.

Call to Action

Sing a song of discipleship.

Incorporate the notion of following Jesus into the prayers and parts of this Mass. For example:

at the penitential rite ("We have failed to follow Jesus..."), at the invitation to communion ("This is Jesus who inspires us to lead wholesome lives. Happy are those..."), and at the solemn blessing ("Go forth to follow Jesus...").

Encourage the children to hang a portrait of Jesus in their room among the pop stars and personalities, and to put up one of Jesus' sayings as well.

Help the children interview two friends who have given some thought to what James and John were thinking.

Fourth Sunday in Ordinary Time

Gospel
A reading from the holy Gospel according to Mark (1:21–28)

They went to Capernaum; and when the sabbath came, he entered the synagogue and taught. They were astounded at his teaching, for he taught them as one having authority, and not as the scribes. Just then there was in their synagogue a man with an unclean spirit, and he cried out, "What have you to do with us, Jesus of Nazareth? Have you come to destroy us? I know who you are, the Holy One of God." But Jesus rebuked him, saying, "Be silent, and come out of him!" And the unclean spirit, convulsing him and crying with a loud voice, came out of him. They were all amazed, and they kept on asking one another, "What is this? A new teaching—with authority! He commands even the unclean spirits, and they obey him." At once his fame began to spread throughout the surrounding region of Galilee.

The gospel of the Lord.

Overview
In the gospel story Mark throws Jesus into battle with evil. Jesus puts evil spirits to flight from a possessed man. Jesus is successful but only after a struggle.

In the liturgy we are invited to join in the struggle on the side of Jesus and all that he stands for. The homilist or teacher, through this story, enriches the children's imagination with the facts and hints at the power struggle between good and evil in the children and in our world.

Focusing Experiences
Think about:

stories about power struggles...

Many of the science fiction/cartoon type stories on children's television programs focus on the struggle between good and evil. It's worth naming and exploring some of these stories.

Exploring the Word of God

Jesus was in the synagogue. He was a traveling preacher and was invited to say a few words to the congregation. And the words came out of him like music, like sunlight. All the people listened. And what he said touched them. It seemed to reach into them.

A scream filled the air. Everyone looked around. A man possessed by an evil spirit stood in the doorway. The man's voice shouted abuse at Jesus.

"We know who you are. You are Jesus of Nazareth." said the voice. "You are God's messenger. Leave us alone."

Jesus walked toward the man, looked him in the eye and confronted the evil spirit that held the man prisoner. The evil spirit went quiet. In a calm, strong voice Jesus told the evil spirit to leave the man. There was a deathly silence. The man shuddered and collapsed as if a great inner force was going out of him. The evil spirit had no more power over him. The man recovered and sat among the people.

There was an explosion of talk and wonderment all around. Everyone was looking at Jesus. Who was he? First, they heard him stand up before them and talk like a prophet of God, then they saw him overcome the evil spirits in the man. Was he the Messiah of God? Was he the one promised by God from ages past?

Call to Faith

May the good forces in us prevail.

May the evil forces in us be conquered.

May Jesus be the great good force in our lives to show us the way to live.

Call to Action

At Mass, speak of the good forces/evil forces at the penitential rite, as an introduction to communion ("We welcome Jesus the great force for good in our lives..."), after communion ("We are fed with the bread of life to be a community that will oppose evil and welcome the ways of Jesus"), and at the final blessing ("We are blessed to go out to make a community where good holds evil in check").

Have the children think of the good and the evil forces in their lives. Resolve to carry out some action to reinforce the good forces and hold the evil forces in check.

Without doubt, one of the great forces in our lives for good or evil is television. This would be good time for a parish to bring in some speakers who can offer help to parents and families on using television wisely.

FIFTH SUNDAY IN ORDINARY TIME

Gospel
A reading from the holy Gospel according to Mark (1:29–39)

As soon as they left the synagogue, they entered the house of Simon and Andrew, with James and John. Now Simon's mother-in-law was in bed with a fever, and they told him about her at once. He came and took her by the hand and lifted her up. Then the fever left her, and she began to serve them.

That evening, at sundown, they brought to him all who were sick or possessed with demons. And the whole city was gathered around the door. And he cured many who were sick with various diseases, and cast out many demons; and he would not permit the demons to speak, because they knew him.

In the morning, while it was still very dark, he got up and went out to a deserted place, and there he prayed.

The gospel of the Lord.

Overview
Jesus is shown to be a man of compassion and prayer. Both qualities connect Jesus in different ways with God. Mark in his gospel works quite hard to show that Jesus shunned publicity. He wasn't a show-off miracle worker. He wasn't show and glitz. Service to others was his role in life.

We should help the children to savor this very human story of the curing of Simon Peter's mother-in-law and the way Jesus handled the publicity.

Focusing Experiences
Everyone is different. Our experience of everyone is different. Our friends are different from one another. They have different personalities, different feelings, different sensitivities. Our friends have strong points—and each friend has different strong points. Jesus had a great sense of compassion. He was full of tenderness. That was one of his strong points.

Jesus also loved to pray. He needed quiet times to do that, and he made quiet times for himself. Some people found it hard to understand why he did that, when he could have been busy making a name for himself.

Exploring the Word of God

James and John went with Jesus to the home of Simon and Andrew. But bad news of a sort awaited them in the house. Simon's mother-in-law was in bed with a fever and she was feeling very poorly. There was gloom in the house and people moved around very quietly.

The problem was that Simon's mother-in-law was very good with people. She was full of stories and had a great way of making people feel welcome. She was much missed when the guests were there. Jesus saw that the house was very empty without her. He went to the sick room. The woman was in a high fever. She looked ghastly, completely washed out.

Jesus took her hand and held it gently and looked at her. She opened her eyes. At that instant the fever seemed to die in her. The color came back into her cheeks, and she smiled. In a few seconds she was out of the bedroom and downstairs to welcome the guests. People said she never looked better.

The whole incident caused much astonishment in the locality. People looked at the woman and looked at Jesus who had cured her. They were full of admiration for Jesus. Long after he went to bed they were still talking about him.

Jesus got up before dawn and went off to a lonely place, stayed there, and settled in to praying to the Father.

In the morning Simon and the others came searching for him to find out where he was. They saw him and they interrupted him to tell him that he was the talk of the land. "Everybody wants to meet you," they said. "Your name is held in high regard. You are a favorite with the people. You're popular. Come back to them. Speak to them. Preach the word to them. Heal them. They are waiting for you." The disciples, who didn't know Jesus all that well yet, wanted him to become famous, to become a big name, a star.

But Jesus didn't go back. He didn't want to go back. The disciples couldn't make sense of all this. They thought he was losing an opportunity to put himself across to the people.

By moving away from all the publicity, Jesus was trying to help them understand that he sometimes needed to be quiet to talk to his Father in heaven.

He continued to pray. Prayer and praying meant a lot to him—more than anyone imagined. Then he said, "Let's move away to a new place." Off they went together, away from the crowds.

Call to Faith

We are called to a deeper understanding of who Jesus is.

We praise him for curing Simon's mother-in-law. We praise him for leading us to pray.

We are called to serve and pray—just like Jesus.

Call to Action

Prayer and praying is a vital Christian activity.

Encourage parents and children to become involved in the prayers of the Mass.

Explain again what the prayer of the faithful is. Ask parents and children to play a part in the prayer of the faithful.

If possible, chant the eucharistic prayer on this occasion.

Pray the Our Father with gestures at this Mass.

Explain that singing in church has been described as praying twice. Sing together now.

Encourage families to become involved in some form of family prayer, even once a week. A variety of possibilities might be suggested.

Sixth Sunday in Ordinary Time

Gospel
A reading from the holy Gospel according to Mark (1:40–45)

A leper came to him begging him, and kneeling he said to him, "If you choose, you can make me clean." Moved with pity, Jesus stretched out his hand and touched him, and said to him, "I do choose. Be made clean!" Immediately the leprosy left him, and he was made clean. After sternly warning him he sent him away at once, saying to him, "See that you say nothing to anyone; but go, show yourself to the priest and offer for your cleansing what Moses commanded, as a testimony to them." But he went out and began to proclaim it freely, and to spread the word, so that Jesus could no longer go into a town openly, but stayed out in the country; and people came to him from every quarter.

The gospel of the Lord.

Overview
The story centers around the cure of a leper. God's love is in action through Jesus. The outcast is welcomed back. The messianic times are with us.

But many people want to be mesmerized by a wonder worker and a healer. Mark goes out of his way to lift Jesus beyond the world of cures and wonder works (the cured man is forbidden to publicize the happy event) and to hint at a destiny that will lead to a cross and the salvation of the world.

We tell this lovely story of a leper cured to the children. It is God's love at work through the gentle touch of Jesus. We end the story with a hint that it is part of a bigger story about Jesus that is being slowly revealed to us.

Focusing Experiences
Dramatize the story through the following play (from *The Columba Lectionary for Masses with Children*). Highlight the fearless way Jesus touched the untouchable leper.

Interviewer	You were a leper?
Leper	I was a leper.
Interviewer	You stood before Jesus. That's against the Law of Moses.
Leper	I took a chance.
Interviewer	You went on your knees before him?
Leper	I did.
Interviewer	He didn't run away from you?
Leper	He's not that kind. He's not afraid of evil, or disease, or anything.
Interviewer	Is it true that he reached out his hands toward you?
Leper	He reached out his hand toward me and he touched me. He touched me.
Interviewer	He touched you, a leper? Some people would say that was foolish, even stupid.
Leper	Maybe it was, but I felt the love of God in his touch. I felt the power of God in that hand that touched me so warmly. I felt new and healed and clean. I was cured. The priest confirmed it.
Interviewer	What are your plans now that you are no longer a leper?
Leper	I have been rescued from a living hell by Jesus. I want to go out and tell people what God's love has done for me. I want other diseased and lonely people to hear Jesus' voice and feel the power of the love of God that Jesus brings everywhere he goes.

A more immediate focusing experience for the homily might center on the way some diseases cause fear or revulsion in others.

Exploring the Word of God

Jesus reached out his hand to touch a leper. Flesh on flesh. People thought it was a dreadful thing to do. Didn't he know that the disease was contagious, that it spread? Wasn't he worried about being infected? Of being struck down with the disease?

He didn't just touch the leper in a hesitant way. He embraced him. He held nothing back. He welcomed the diseased man back to the world of people. He drew the outcast near his own warm heart. His touch was full of love—so full of love that it cured the leper. The disease left the man. He became as healthy as you or me. The leper was one of the people again. The leper's dream of coming in from the cold, from the world of outcasts, had come true.

Jesus told the leper to say nothing because Jesus didn't want publicity. But he might as well have been talking to the wall. The leper went around advertising Jesus, the wonderfully kind man who cured him.

When the word spread around about the cure of the leper, everyone wanted to find out more about Jesus. Some people said he had strange powers. Some people said he had cures. Some people said he was a wonder worker. Some people had faith and were saying, "He is the Messiah for sure."

The excitement was unbelievable. Jesus had to hide out in the desert away from towns and villages. Too many people were looking for a wonder worker.

He wanted people to know that he was the Messiah sent by God. Many of them weren't ready for this news yet.

Call to Faith

Jesus, you touched the leper with God's love.
> You healed the leper with the power of God that was in you.
> You made the leper feel welcome again.
> Jesus, you are the Messiah of God; we believe in you.
> God our Father, make us gentle as Jesus was gentle.
> Make us compassionate as Jesus was compassionate.
> Touch us with love to make us gentle and loving.

Call to Action

Sing songs of faith in Jesus.

At Mass, an expression of faith in Jesus, the bread of life, would also be appropriate at communion.

Seventh Sunday in Ordinary Time

Gospel
A reading from the holy Gospel according to Mark (2:1–12)

When he returned to Capernaum after some days, it was reported that he was at home. So many gathered around that there was no longer room for them, not even in front of the door; and he was speaking the word to them. Then some people came, bringing to him a paralyzed man, carried by four of them. And when they could not bring him to Jesus because of the crowd, they removed the roof above him; and after having dug through it, they let down the mat on which the paralytic lay. When Jesus saw their faith, he said to the paralytic, "Son, your sins are forgiven." Now some of the scribes were sitting there, questioning in their hearts, "Why does this fellow speak in this way? It is blasphemy! Who can forgive sins but God alone?" At once Jesus perceived in his spirit that they were discussing these questions among themselves; and he said to them, "Why do you raise such questions in your hearts? Which is easier, to say to the paralytic, 'Your sins are forgiven,' or to say, 'Stand up and take your mat and walk'? But so that you may know that the Son of Man has authority on earth to forgive sins"—he said to the paralytic—"I say to you, stand up, take your mat and go to your home." And he stood up, and immediately took the mat and went out before all of them; so that they were all amazed and glorified God, saying, "We have never seen anything like this!"

The gospel of the Lord.

Overview
Love is shown here to be very practical. Their friend was a cripple in a stretcher. They were prepared to go to the ends of the earth to help him—well, at least to stripping a roof to lower him, stretcher and all, to the feet of Jesus. Jesus brought God's love to this crippled man to release him from his disability. Jesus also touched the man's soul with God's love and forgiveness. This, more than anything, caused a stir. It

was a clear messianic sign. It was a challenge for those who didn't recognize Jesus. It was a claim to be opposed, an outrage to be condemned. It went against the way these experts read and understood sacred history. They opposed Jesus. They were very vocal in their opposition.

We don't argue the theological case for what Jesus is doing. We simply present Jesus to the children as a channel of God's love. He heals the crippled man. He also heals hearts. He opens a way for people to come back into God's love.

Focusing Experiences
Ask the children to think about forgiveness, especially the forgiveness of parents. It means a lot when outraged parents say it is OK, to forget it. It is wonderful when parents make the effort to say it is all right, even when we have shamed them, let them down, made them look foolish, done something dreadful. It is special to still feel loved even though what we have done deserves heavy sanctions. We are loved and forgiven. Forgiveness is a kind of healing. If parents couldn't bring themselves to forgive, then a kind of wound is left unhealed.

When God gives us forgiveness a kind of healing is going on. Love heals us and makes us feel right again. It is such a lovely feeling.

Exploring the Word of God
Jesus was in a house in Capernaum. The crowds followed him there. Every room filled up with people. The room where Jesus was speaking was particularly crowded. There wasn't an an inch of space, but no one seemed to mind. They were where they wanted to be. Some men came toward the house carrying a friend on a stretcher. He was crippled. They tried to bring their friend in to Jesus to be cured, but there was no room. They had to stay outside.

As Jesus was speaking there was a slight tearing noise in the roof. Daylight began to stream in through a space in the roof timbers. A man's face appeared in the opening. The people below could see two or three other men on the roof. Jesus stopped speaking to watch what was happening. The men on the roof stripped more roof covering from the timbers overhead. The opening was now quite large, like a big trap door. A stretcher on the roof was maneuvered into the space, and a crippled man was lowered down to where Jesus was. Everyone was amazed at what was happening.

Jesus bent over the crippled man: "Your sins are forgiven," he said. That caused a great stir. These words were sacred words. Some religious leaders were present and they rebuked Jesus: "You are not entitled to say those words. It is not allowed. Forgiveness of sin is not in your giving. It is God who forgives sins."

"You don't believe I have God's power to forgive sins," Jesus replied. "Neither do you believe that I have God's power to say to this crippled man: 'Rise up and walk.'"

"No! we don't believe that," they said.

"Maybe," said Jesus. "If he rises out of this bed and walks, you will also believe that I have God's power to forgive sin, so I say to this crippled man, stand up and move from your stretcher. Get up and walk."

The man did as he was told. He moved withered legs that now were full of life and energy. He stood up and walked.

There was silence...then astonishment...then consternation as everyone spoke at the same time.

It seemed to everyone that Jesus had power from God to heal. And if he had power from God to heal then he also had power to forgive sin.

Many people believed in him and followed him.

Call to Faith

Jesus, you bring us God's love.

Jesus, you bring us God's love to make things good for us.

You bring us God's love to take away our faults.

You bring us God's love to make us better friends.

You bring us God's love to show us a new way to live.

Jesus, you heal us and you reconcile us.

Jesus, you bring us God's love to show us a way of harmony and peace.

Call to Action

Make arrangements for a penance service. On this occasion arrange for each participant to have a personal counseling time.

EIGHTH SUNDAY IN ORDINARY TIME

Gospel
A reading from the holy Gospel according to Mark (2:18–22)

Now John's disciples and the Pharisees were fasting; and people came and said to Jesus, "Why do John's disciples and the disciples of the Pharisees fast, but your disciples do not fast?" Jesus said to them, "The wedding guests cannot fast while the bridegroom is with them, can they? As long as they have the bridegroom with them, they cannot fast. The days will come when the bridegroom is taken away from them, and then they will fast on that day.

"No one sews a piece of unshrunk cloth on an old cloak; otherwise, the patch pulls away from it, the new from the old, and a worse tear is made. And no one puts new wine into old wineskins; otherwise, the wine will burst the skins, and the wine is lost, and so are the skins; but one puts new wine into fresh wineskins."

The gospel of the Lord.

Overview
In the days of Jesus many people had a high regard for fasting. It was a good way to show respect for God. It was a good way to be quiet before God. It was a good way to get the the body in tune with God.

But Jesus was the biggest thing God had ever ever done for the people. The only way to show regard for what God had done was to celebrate and praise God. Anything else was too little and too dull. Fasting didn't measure up. Celebrating did.

As always, the children need to be helped to savor the details of the story to build up their own picture of Jesus. Jesus is someone worth celebrating.

Focusing Experiences
Sing some celebration songs.

Introduce the homily with a celebration song honoring Jesus.

Exploring the Word of God
In the days of Jesus everyone seemed to be fasting. John the Baptist's disciples were fasting. They sometimes went a whole day without food.

It was their way of showing they were serious about God. Food was not their master, God was. They put up with hunger to show they loved God more than anything.

The disciples of the Pharisees were fasting. They had rules about the times to fast and the places to fast, rules about the weight of food you could eat if you were doing a light fast, rules about a big fast, rules about the amount of water allowed during the fast, rules about the clothes you wore during the fast, rules about the way you sat, rules about the prayers you said before, during and after the fast. Some people thought there were too many rules, but they didn't like to say too much. They didn't like to speak out.

Those for whom fasting was a way of life spoke out against the disciples of Jesus. "How come," they asked, "the disciples of Jesus don't fast? They mustn't think much about God."

Jesus turned to those who were complaining about his disciples. "Tell me something," he said. "Is it right to accept an invitation to a wedding and then refuse the food offered at the celebration because you are doing a fast? You couldn't do that. It would be hurtful. A wedding celebration isn't the time for fasting. It is a time for joy, for sitting round the table and eating a celebration meal with the bride and groom.

"If someone close to you were getting married would you spoil the day by fasting? No food? No music? No songs? No dancing? Wouldn't it be terrible! What a gloomy day for the young couple! If you were an attendant to the bridegroom, would you fast? You'd spoil the day for everybody."

A few people began to take in what Jesus was getting at.

Jesus was saying that there is a time for everything—a time when God's people fast, a time when God's people celebrate, a time for keeping quiet, a time when God's people sing out their praise and thanks.

And Jesus left them in no doubt that he meant exactly that. "These are new days," he said. "It's a time to celebrate God's goodness. The bridegroom is with you. God has touched you in a new way. God is walking among you. It's a time to praise God for everything that is happening. It's a time to give thanks. It's a time to be glad, and glad we will be."

Jesus and the disciples went down the road singing and praising God.

Call to Faith
We must celebrate Jesus now!
We must celebrate Jesus in our words.
We must celebrate Jesus in our songs.

We must celebrate Jesus in our processions with color and banners.
We must celebrate Jesus in our hearts.

Call to Action

Today is an opportunity to celebrate Jesus with songs, words, flowers,
candles, banners, a procession, and music.

Ninth Sunday in Ordinary Time

Gospel
A reading from the holy Gospel according to Mark (2:23–3:6)

One sabbath Jesus was going through the grainfields; and as they made their way his disciples began to pluck heads of grain. The Pharisees said to him, "Look, why are they doing what is not lawful on the sabbath?" And he said to them, "Have you never read what David did when he and his companions were hungry and in need of food? He entered the house of God, when Abiathar was high priest, and ate the bread of the Presence, which it is not lawful for any but the priests to eat, and he gave some to his companions." Then he said to them, "The sabbath was made for humankind, and not humankind for the sabbath; so the Son of Man is lord even of the sabbath."

Again he entered the synagogue, and a man was there who had a withered hand. They watched him to see whether he would cure him on the sabbath, so that they might accuse him. And he said to the man who had the withered hand, "Come forward." Then he said to them, "Is it lawful to do good or to do harm on the sabbath, to save life or to kill?" But they were silent. He looked around at them with anger; he was grieved at their hardness of heart and said to the man, "Stretch out your hand." He stretched it out, and his hand was restored. The Pharisees went out and immediately conspired with the Herodians against him, how to destroy him.

The gospel of the Lord.

Overview
Another argument about fasting. Jesus lays down the law about fasting! But laying down the law is the job of a prophet. Who does Jesus think he is? Jesus' action in interpreting the Law is very significant and very threatening to those who have no faith in him.

This story will help the children to see Jesus as the one who puts us right about God and about the way God's love works.

Focusing Experiences

We adults say (in our best moments) that love should come first. We call it the primacy of charity. We don't always succeed in getting it right, but it is a good principle.

We might ask the children if they feel love should come first.

At home, if someone is feeling hurt or down or in need of encouragement, that has to come first—before homework assignments or parents' schedules, or anything else.

At school, if someone needs a bit of comfort or personal counseling, that has to take precedence over other things that seem important—such as rules of punctuality or class attendance or assignments. Otherwise we don't put love first.

Exploring the Word of God

People we know often chew sweets or gum or tobacco or even the end of a pen or pencil.

In the days of Jesus people often chewed a kernel of corn. It was the custom. It was what they did. It was a habit that passed the time.

There were people who said it is all right to chew the kernel on a Monday or Tuesday or Wednesday but not on the sabbath. It was forbidden to do it on a sabbath. They said it was against God's Law. And these people always seemed to be coming up with things that were against God's Law. Their ideas became rules of sabbath observance. Anyone who broke the rules of sabbath observance got an earful!

Jesus' disciples were seen chewing kernels of corn on the sabbath. They thought they'd never hear the end of it. What a lecture they got.

It was bad enough eating corn kernels on a sabbath, but when Jesus cured a man in the synagogue who had a useless hand and did it on the sabbath, there was no end to the complaints. Jesus heard what they were saying. He had a few words of his own to say to these narrow-minded people. "Hey," he said, "is there to be no mercy on the sabbath, no forgiveness, no healing of bodies or of hearts, no acts of generosity, no kindnesses on the sabbath? God is a God of love. God wants you to show love for your neighbor on a Monday, and on the sabbath. Don't put a damper on God's love. Put God's love to work every day. Don't hold back. God's way is the way of love every day of the week."

And he left them there to think that over, and went on his way with the disciples.

The sabbath rules people were very angry with him and began to plot to get rid of him.

Call to Faith

Jesus you bring us God's love.
>You are God's voice for us.
>You are God's wisdom to us.
>You are God's love bringing us closer to God.
>We believe in you. We follow you.

Call to Action

Ask the children to collect stories from television, newspapers, and magazines on people who put love first.

Ask someone in a child care role to speak to the children about how they try to put love first.

Offer testimony from a parent about love at home.

Offer testimony from a teacher about love at school.

Offer testimony from a priest or pastoral minister about love in pastoral work.

Incorporate the slogan "Put Love First" into various parts of the Mass, for example, into the penitential rite ("We failed to put love first..."), invitation to communion ("This is Jesus who put love first. Happy are those..."), and solemn blessing ("Go forth in peace to put love first...").

TENTH SUNDAY IN ORDINARY TIME

Gospel
A reading from the holy Gospel according to Mark (3:20–35)

Then Jesus went home; and the crowd came together again, so that they could not even eat. When his family heard it, they went out to restrain him, for people were saying, "He has gone out of his mind." And the scribes who came down from Jerusalem said, "He has Beelzebul, and by the ruler of the demons he casts out demons." And he called them to him, and spoke to them in parables, "How can Satan cast out Satan? If a kingdom is divided against itself, that kingdom cannot stand. And if a house is divided against itself, that house will not be able to stand. And if Satan has risen up against himself and is divided, he cannot stand, but his end has come."

The gospel of the Lord.

Overview
In Mark's gospel we never really get away from viewing the portrait of Jesus. In each story we are invited to look again, and something new is pointed out to feed our faith and our belief. In today's gospel we are invited to look again and dismiss the smears that Jesus is really in league with the devil.

The children should enjoy today's story. It makes a spirited stand for Jesus' reputation.

Focusing Experiences
Think about:
    running campaigns
    smear campaigns
    rumor mongering
    working on people's fears

Exploring the Word of God
The news of Jesus and what he was doing and saying was spreading everywhere. The talk on everyone's lips was about Jesus. People couldn't get over how openly he spoke about God. He seemed to know so much about God. No one had ever talked like this about God before.

He spoke as if God was his close friend. He called God "Father." He spoke as if he knew what was in God's mind. Some listened to what he had to say and thought it was the best news they ever heard. They believed in Jesus and followed him.

What Jesus was saying and doing, however, did not go down well with a small group of powerful people. They thought it was an outrage that Jesus should make himself out to be close to God, should be speaking for God, and telling people what God wanted them to do. They were furious with Jesus and wanted him silenced.

They approached his relatives in Nazareth and worked on their fears and their respect for God. "If you, good people, have any respect for God," they said, "you will stop Jesus from talking about God. Jesus is making a fool of himself. He's out of his depth. He's not God's special friend. He's not God's voice to the people. His actions and his preaching must be an embarrassment to decent people like yourselves. It's obvious he's had some kind of breakdown. He's sick. He doesn't know what he is saying. He needs looking after. He's getting you talked about and giving you a bad name. If he goes on like this you won't be able to hold up your head in the community. No one will speak to you. You won't be able to take your place among the people at the synagogue. Take him home and talk sense to him. Don't allow him to even as much as mention the name of God again. You have the family's good to think about." They went on and on like that until Jesus' relatives were really worried about Jesus.

They decided to go to where Jesus was speaking and bring him home. They thought it best to take him into their care, to mind him and look after him until he got over whatever kind of breakdown he was suffering.

In the meantime the powerful people who were against Jesus were also doing their best to spread a rumor that Jesus was possessed by a devil. They gave out a story that he was possessed by Beelzebul, the prince of devils. That explained, they said, how he spoke so well and how he cured people. He has devil's magic! But nobody was willing to listen to that story. The people reasoned that if Jesus had the devil in him, how come he was always trying to spread love and put an end to evil? They wanted an answer to that. They wanted to know why he was turning people back to God. "Devils are supposed to turn you away from God," they said to Jesus' enemies. "Look at the numbers who have turned back to God. Your story doesn't make any sense. What's more, Jesus is a power for good. It's not the devil that's in him, it's God. For all we know he might be the Messiah."

When those who were opposed to Jesus heard it suggested that Jesus might be the Messiah of God, they got very angry indeed and rushed off to think up more conspiracies against him.

In the meantime Jesus escaped quietly from his relations and quickly left his home town to go to other towns and villages to spread the good news about God's love.

Call to Faith

Jesus, you weren't out of your mind.
> You are out of the ordinary.
> You are out of this world.
> Some people don't recognize you and that is a pity.
> We recognize you.
> We accept you as God's voice among us.
> We praise and thank God for all that you are to us.
> You are Jesus, God's beloved Son.
> We are your followers, and we love you.

Call to Action

The emphasis in today's Mass might be on our meeting with Jesus—Mass as our meeting with Jesus. The theme of this Mass as a meeting with Jesus might be expanded in the introduction and highlighted in the various parts of the Mass that follow. Songs might be found to follow this theme.

Eleventh Sunday in Ordinary Time

Gospel
A reading from the holy gospel according to Mark (4:26–34)

Jesus also said, "With what can we compare the kingdom of God, or what parable will we use for it? It is like a mustard seed, which, when sown upon the ground, is the smallest of all the seeds on earth; yet when it is sown it grows up and becomes the greatest of all shrubs, and puts forth large branches, so that the birds of the air can make nests in its shade."

The gospel of the Lord.

Overview
This parable gave hope to adult Christians in Mark's day who were feeling under threat of extinction. For children it is advisable to present the parable as an answer to the wider question, "Can God's love spread in the world?" They will understand the issue involved and where Jesus is leading in the parable.

Focusing Experiences
Have a nature walk among giant trees. Admire their growth and strength.

Explore some reasons for the spread of:
particular types of music
styles of dress
styles of art
styles of building

Exploring the Word of God
Jesus had a story for people who wondered about the spread of God's love. Can it reach out across the world? Can God's love spread? Can it grow?

Can God's love move out of people's hearts into the streets, into the cities, across the land? Is the power of God buried quietly in people, or does it come alive in a way that allows love, peace, generosity, and justice to spread far and wide? It was a great question, and Jesus took it up.

Think about a seed, he said. It's small. It's hidden. It lies in the ground. But it comes alive in the ground. A few small roots search the ground for food. The seed becomes a plant. It feeds. It drinks. It grows. It breaks through the ground and faces wind and frost. It survives and grows strong. It grows and grows. It becomes a tree. In time it becomes a mighty tree, standing tall and reaching into the sky. Once a seed, hidden, buried, small, and weak—now a great tree spreading its branches over the ground.

The disciples knew what Jesus was saying. God's love mustn't stay quietly in our hearts. It must spread out of people's hearts into the streets, into the cities, across the land. In a way it must fill the earth.

Call to Faith

God, our Father, your love is strong.
Your love spreads and grows through Jesus.
Your love spreads and grows through us.
It takes our hearts to nurture it.
It takes our hands and our feet to make it spread.
It takes our actions to bring it to new places.
It takes our commitment to keep it alive.

We are called to be part of the effort to spread God's love.
We are called to make a commitment to spread God's love.
We are called to be active in spreading God's love.

Call to Action

Parents, teachers, priests, and missionaries are the great spreaders of God's love. Highlight their roles.

Invite a Christian worker with experience in spreading the seed of God's love in another country to speak briefly.

Twelfth Sunday in Ordinary Time

Gospel
A reading from the holy Gospel according to Mark (4:35–41)

On that day, when evening had come, Jesus said to them, "Let us go across to the other side." And leaving the crowd behind, they took him with them in the boat, just as he was. Other boats were with him. A great windstorm arose, and the waves beat into the boat, so that the boat was already being swamped. But he was in the stern, asleep on the cushion; and they woke him up and said to him, "Teacher, do you not care that we are perishing?" He woke up and rebuked the wind, and said to the sea, "Peace! Be still!" Then the wind ceased, and there was a dead calm. He said to them, "Why are you afraid? Have you still no faith?" And they were filled with great awe and said to one another, "Who then is this, that even the wind and the sea obey him?"

The gospel of the Lord.

Overview
The disciples are in a boat. The storm is tossing them about and they are afraid. Jesus saves them.

Here are the headlines about Jesus from this story: He saves his friends. His friends can depend on him. He will be there in moments of crisis. He will be looking out for us.

This story allows the children's imagination to run riot! Jesus the hero will figure strongly in the desperate situations in which they imagine themselves on the Sea of Galilee.

Focusing Experiences
Think of:
desperate situations
masterful rescues
being rescued by a friend

Exploring the Word of God

Jesus and his disciples were in a boat on the Sea of Galilee. Jesus fell asleep. The others took turns with the rowing. A wind stirred up—a strong wind. It whipped up the water and made big waves. It was heavy work rowing. The only course of action was to stop rowing and run with the wind. The disciples kept the nose of the boat into the waves and ploughed their way through the water. The storm got worse, and they became frightened. They were into a full gale. The boat was buffeted by huge waves. The sea became a monster lifting them up on a big wave and dropping them off the crest into a deep trough. Each time their boat fell they expected to be swallowed up in the water. At the last minute the boat seemed to be lifted again and they were made to wait for death with the next drop.

The disciples were lying in the well of the boat being sloshed about in dirty water, dead fish, and fishing gear that had come loose. They were holding on to whatever they could to avoid being swept overboard, waiting for the worst as the boat rose and fell. They didn't know if Jesus was still asleep or dead. But someone had the presence of mind to call out to him. "Jesus, save us!! We are perishing! Jesus, Jesus, help us."

Suddenly, the boat stopped heaving up and down. The wind died away to a whisper and the raging sea became calm. The disciples picked themselves up from the floor of the boat and began to row again. It was a miracle. It had to be. When they talked about it afterward, when they went ashore, someone remembered seeing Jesus standing in the prow of the boat with his hands outstretched over the raging water in a calming gesture. The more they thought about it and the more they talked about it they came to the strong belief that God had given Jesus power over wind and wave. But more than that—he had come to their aid when they needed him. And that they would never forget. They all went off quietly to praise and thank God for Jesus.

Call to Faith

Jesus, you are our friend.
> You want to be our friend.
> You are always looking out for us.
> You are there when we need you.
> You won't let us down.
> You will save us.
> You will be our comfort in times of distress.
> You will be our savior in times of peril.
> You will be our friend at all times.

Call to Action

Emphasize Jesus our Friend. At Mass, a large banner with that title could add to the decoration and the celebration of Jesus as friend. With songs and prayers on this theme the children could grow in friendship with Jesus.

Colorful drawings of the disciples in the storm could decorate classrooms or homes.

Thirteenth Sunday in Ordinary Time

Gospel
A reading from the holy Gospel according to Mark (5:21–43)

When Jesus had crossed again in the boat to the other side, a great crowd gathered around him; and he was by the sea. Then one of the leaders of the synagogue named Jairus came and, when he saw him, fell at his feet and begged him repeatedly, "My little daughter is at the point of death. Come and lay your hands on her, so that she may be made well, and live." So he went with him.

And a large crowd followed him and pressed in on him.

Some people came from the leader's house to say, "Your daughter is dead. Why trouble the teacher any further?" But overhearing what they had said, Jesus said to the leader of the synagogue, "Do not fear, only believe." He allowed no one to follow him except Peter, James, and John, the brother of James. When they came to the house of the leader of the synagogue, he saw a commotion, people weeping and wailing loudly. When he had entered, he said to them, "Why do you make a commotion and weep? The child is not dead but sleeping." And they laughed at him. Then he put them all outside, and took the child's father and mother and those who were with him, and went in where the child was. He took her by the hand and said to her, "Talitha cum," which means, "Little girl, get up!" And immediately the girl got up and began to walk about (she was twelve years of age). At this they were overcome with amazement. He strictly ordered them that no one should know this, and told them to give her something to eat.

The gospel of the Lord.

Overview
On this Sunday we hear about Jairus, a very worried father whose daughter is close to death. We share the feelings of hope when the fa-

ther goes to Jesus, of despair when the news comes through that the girl is dead, then finally the great joy of her reunion with the family.

An underlying message embedded in this story is that children are safe with God, even in death. God has power over death. God can reach across the divide and keep them safe in death. It is a consoling thought for families who have lost a child to death. These children are safe with God. God rescues them from the paralysis of death. We may never see them again in this world, but they are safe and at home with God.

Focusing Experiences
One might be able to recall with sensitivity the death of a child—the terrible loss parents and family feel, the grief, loneliness, and emptiness. One might be able to hint at the support some parents and family feel with the thought that their child is safe with God even in death, that God's love reaches across death to comfort the child.

Exploring the Word of God
Jairus' daughter was desperately ill and showed no signs of recovery. The news was bad. She was getting worse by the hour. Everyone in the house was very worried. Jairus was a man of faith and made up his mind to go himself and plead with Jesus to come and cure her. So he went and met up with Jesus. Jairus described his daughter and told Jesus of the sickness that had taken hold of her that would surely steal her life away. He said he was a man of faith and knew Jesus could cure her. Jesus said he would answer a request made with such strong faith.

While they were on the road messengers arrived from Jairus' house to say that the young girl had died during the night. Jairus was heartbroken. Through his tears he excused Jesus from traveling any further. "Everyone will understand," he said. "There's nothing more any of us can do."

But Jesus continued on to the house encouraging Jairus to have faith in God. When he arrived at the house everyone was in mourning. He said, "Please don't grieve, she is not dead, she is sleeping." Accompanied by the girl's mother and father and his own disciples he went to the room where the dead girl lay. He looked at her with great love. He took the little girl by the hand and said, "Talitha cum, little girl, I say to you, wake up."

Outside the room there was silence. Everyone in the house was waiting. Every eye watched the bedroom door. Then the door opened and the girl stood in the doorway with her mother and father beside her. The whole place came to life. Such excitement! Such talk! Such celebration! The questions in everybody's mind were: How did Jesus do it? How did he have power over death? What was the meaning of this event? Who was he? Where did he get his power. How was he connected with God?

Was Jesus the Messiah promised by God to the people from ages past? It was a wonderful thought. So exciting! But was it possible? His disciples and the people in Jairus' house said openly that Jesus was the Messiah. They had faith. They could see things behind the scenes. And they thanked God for showing them that God's friends were safe and well looked after even in death.

Call to Faith

Jesus, you are kind and good.
> You listened to Jairus who had a sick daughter.
> You listen to our parents when they are worried.
> You listen to people who have faith and trust in God.
> You listen to us and we know you hear us.
> We feel safe with God because you teach us to love and admire God.
> We know that those who have died are safe in God's care.
> That is a wonderful thought that makes us very happy.

Call to Action

Parents who have lost a child might find it helpful to express faith in the beautifully consoling thought that their child is safe with God even in death.

Following the theme of feeling safe with God in death, all might be consoled by praying for children (or friends) who have died and whom we feel are safe with God.

Fourteenth Sunday
in Ordinary Time

Gospel
A reading from the holy Gospel according to Mark (6:1–6)

Jesus left that place and came to his hometown, and his disciples followed him. On the sabbath he began to teach in the synagogue, and many who heard him were astounded. They said, "Where did this man get all this? What is this wisdom that has been given to him? What deeds of power are being done by his hands! Is not this the carpenter, the son of Mary and brother of James and Joses and Judas and Simon, and are not his sisters here with us?" And they took offense at him. Then Jesus said to them, "Prophets are not without honor, except in their hometown, and among their own kin, and in their own house." And he could do no deed of power there, except that he laid his hands on a few sick people and cured them. And he was amazed at their unbelief.

The gospel of the Lord.

Overview
It is opposition again for Jesus. His own find it difficult to accept him. He is highly thought of in Nazareth, but they don't have faith in him, cannot accept him as a spokesman for God. That would be an embarrassment. Too big a leap...too much...impossible. It's just too big a challenge.

This story will challenge the children in their own way to accept Jesus and have faith in him.

Focusing Experiences
Ask the children:

Are you ever surprised when your own brothers and sisters and friends seem surprised by your successes?

Are you sometimes surprised by the successes of a brother, sister, or friend?

Exploring the Word of God

His relations and neighbors were astonished to hear Jesus speak so well. He was the guest speaker in the synagogue. Everyone gave him their attention. You couldn't help listening to him. It was the way he spoke and the words he used. He touched you with his words. He had a way of linking into your mind. When you heard him speak you felt you wanted to hear more.

After he had spoken and after the final prayers were said the people gathered outside the synagogue to talk together and share the news of the day. It was Jesus that people were talking about. Someone said that he must be a prophet. His neighbors were quick to squash that idea. "He's not a prophet," they said. "He's too ordinary. We know him. He's one of us. We grew up with him. He showed no signs of being a prophet then. He's not a prophet!"

Someone else pointed out that Jesus was a healer. Maybe his healing power came from God. "He's not a healer," his neighbors said. "He doesn't have power from God. Wouldn't we know? We would be the first to notice. He has cured some people, that's for sure. But don't get carried away by a few strange happenings. One swallow doesn't make a summer! He doesn't have any more power than the rest of us. He's good, but he's ordinary. There's nothing special here. There is no question of God setting him apart for a great mission. Our neighbor Jesus," they said, "should stop talking about God and get on with his life, like the rest of us."

Jesus happened to overhear something of what his neighbors were saying. He was disappointed and got ready to move away from them and on to the next town. As he left he was heard to say, "It's hard to be a prophet in your own town."

Call to Faith

Jesus, our friend, we are sorry that things didn't work out in Nazareth, your hometown.
It is hard to be accepted by your own people. They look for faults.
It seems to be the same everywhere.
Jesus, we accept you.
We believe in you.
We know that you bring God's love to us.
We thank you for everything you do for us.
We are glad to meet you at Mass.
May the friendship between us live and grow today and always.

Call to Action

Slogans like *We accept Jesus* might be used at Mass today. We might stand for Jesus, raise our hands aloft for Jesus, and make other symbolic signs that we accept Jesus. The final blessing might be anticipated by a faith question: Do you accept Jesus?

Fifteenth Sunday in Ordinary Time

Gospel
A reading from the holy Gospel according to Mark (6:7–13)

He called the twelve and began to send them out two by
two, and gave them authority over the unclean spirits. He
ordered them to take nothing for their journey except a
staff; no bread, no bag, no money in their belts; but to wear
sandals and not to put on two tunics. He said to them,
"Wherever you enter a house, stay there until you leave the
place. If any place will not welcome you and they refuse to
hear you, as you leave, shake off the dust that is on your
feet as a testimony against them." So they went out and
proclaimed that all should repent. They cast out many demons, and anointed with oil many who were sick and
cured them.

The gospel of the Lord.

Overview
It's a time for mission. It's a time to say that missionary work cannot
and shouldn't be complicated or compromised by commercial or personal considerations. The work of Jesus requires single-mindedness
and dedication. It's a tall order. We know the ideal. We have to work at
it. We have to be called to do it.

The story will have its own bits and pieces for the children. They'll
chew at it and get thoughts and questions about God and Jesus and the
work of spreading the good news.

Exploring the Word of God
Jesus sent the twelve disciples out to spread the word of God.

How many were to go in each group?

Two by two he sent them, for companionship and friendship, for
strength and for courage.

And what about arrangements for staying overnight?

He told them to keep it simple. Stay in the one house. Moving from
house to house would mean too many meals of welcome and too much
fuss. Keep it simple, he told them.

And what about money for the journey, food, and extra clothes?

"Bring nothing," he said. "Nothing extra at all. You are in God's hands. Trust God. You will be well looked after. Money and clothes and food must not be a worry. They mustn't cross your mind."

And what if the people of a town rejected them? Should they put a curse on that town?

His advice to them was to scrape the dust of that place off their feet to show their hurt feelings to the townspeople and then be on their way. Don't waste time talking to people whose hearts are made of stone. Leave them alone. Move on.

With all this advice and with his blessing they went on their way to towns and villages to spread the word of God.

Call to Faith

We want the good news about Jesus to spread!

We want parents to tell us about Jesus.

We want teachers to explain to us about Jesus.

We want priests and the community to celebrate Jesus with us.

Call to Action

Confirmation is a missionary moment. We are confirmed to be witnesses. This may be a good time now to renew confirmation commitments.

Are there persons in the parish who have a missionary role? This would be a time to give them a platform to express their faith and hopes.

Sixteenth Sunday in Ordinary Time

Gospel
A reading from the holy Gospel according to Mark (6:30–34)

The apostles gathered around Jesus, and told him all that they had done and taught. He said to them, "Come away to a deserted place all by yourselves and rest a while." For many were coming and going, and they had no leisure even to eat. And they went away in the boat to a deserted place by themselves. Now many saw them going and recognized them, and they hurried there on foot from all the towns and arrived ahead of them. As he went ashore, he saw a great crowd; and he had compassion for them, because they were like sheep without a shepherd; and he began to teach them many things.

The gospel of the Lord.

Overview
Today's gospel story puts a high value on meditation. There is a time to be quiet. There is a time to walk and talk with Jesus in the imagination. There is a time to be with Jesus in the mind or heart, enjoying his friendship.

Focusing Experiences
Walk in the country or in the park with the children. Find a peaceful spot. Be silent for awhile listening to sounds. Then be at home in your imagination. And then be at home with the memory.

Exploring the Word of God
The twelve apostles came back from their travels full of excitement, full of good news, with plenty of stories to tell of where they went and who they met on their journeys. Everywhere they went they said the name of Jesus was given a welcome.

In the middle of all this excitement, before they had finished all their stories, Jesus invited them to be at peace, to come away to a quiet place and sit in solitude with God. He often did this himself—slipped away to a quiet place to be with God. Now with their first missionary journey behind them he wanted them to know that quiet times with God were very precious and should be part of their lives.

This morning at this time, I want you young people to join Jesus and the apostles in a quiet place. Imagine the place: Is it a quiet hollow in the mountain? Is it a clearing in the forest? Is it a sand dune in the desert? You choose. You are there with Jesus and his friends.

Bow your heads and maybe even close your eyes. You are loved, deeply loved by God. God really loves you.

Remember a time when you felt very close to your father or to your mother. Remember the details—where you were and what was said.

Remember another time when you felt especially loved. Go through it again in your mind. Bring all the details into focus.

Remember a time when you were with your parents and family and it felt really good. You felt at home, comfortable, at peace.

Know that God loves you with a tremendous love. Open yourself to God's love. Be thankful for God's love. Feel good that God loves you.

Now open your eyes again and hear the song *The Lord is my Shepherd*.

Call to Faith
We are called to walk with Jesus in our minds and in our imagination.

Call to Action
During this Mass we should make an effort to introduce several moments of silence and several pieces of reflective music. This will encourage a positive attitude of reflection among the children.

Seventeenth Sunday
in Ordinary Time

Gospel
A reading from the holy Gospel according to John (6:1–15)

After this Jesus went to the other side of the Sea of Galilee, also called the Sea of Tiberias. A large crowd kept following him, because they saw the signs that he was doing for the sick. Jesus went up the mountain and sat down there with his disciples. Now the Passover, the festival of the Jews, was near. When he looked up and saw a large crowd coming toward him, Jesus said to Philip, "Where are we to buy bread for these people to eat?" He said this to test him, for he himself knew what he was going to do. Philip answered him, "Six months' wages would not buy enough bread for each of them to get a little." One of his disciples, Andrew, Simon Peter's brother, said to him, "There is a boy here who has five barley loaves and two fish. But what are they among so many people?" Jesus said, "Make the people sit down." Now there was a great deal of grass in the place; so they sat down, about five thousand in all. Then Jesus took the loaves, and when he had given thanks, he distributed them to those who were seated; so also the fish, as much as they wanted. When they were satisfied, he told his disciples, "Gather up the fragments left over, so that nothing may be lost." So they gathered them up, and from the fragments of the five barley loaves, left by those who had eaten, they filled twelve baskets. When the people saw the sign that he had done, they began to say, "This is indeed the prophet who is to come into the world."

When Jesus realized that they were about to come and take him by force to make him king, he withdrew again to the mountain by himself.

The gospel of the Lord.

Overview

The gospel reading of today is a story, and telling it as a story will have a great impact on the children. The teacher or homilist must become a storyteller. That means letting the story work through your own imagination first and then regaling the children with all the little curious turns and twists and word pictures that make the story live for you.

Focusing Experiences

This is a time for bread—all kinds of bread. It's a time for looking at bread and linking bread with people of every generation—bread like it was baked years ago, or in biblical times.

A short talk and demonstration from a parishioner who happens to be a baker with a feel for history would be an excellent introduction to this miracle of bread.

We should also hint, by way of immediate introduction to the homily, that bread is a solace for hunger, but also a symbol of friendship, a symbol of community, a symbol of love.

Exploring the Word of God

Five thousand hungry people were gathered together. Yes, five thousand. All of them had been there hour after hour with Jesus...walking in the sun...feeling the heat...and putting an effort into listening to him. They were as hungry as you would expect them to be. And they were tired. Jesus said something had to be done for them. The disciples found a boy in the crowd who wanted to share his lunch of five barley loaves and two fishes. It wouldn't go very far but it was something.

Jesus took the bread and blessed it and asked the disciples to share it with the people. He also asked them to share the fish. It doesn't make sense but it happened. Five thousand hungry people were fed with the five loaves and two fishes. All of them were fed, and there was bread left over.

The people were all trying to figure out what happened. Everyone could see that it was some kind of miracle, a miracle of bread. It wasn't just about hungry people getting fed. Some people felt there was more to it than that. It was a miracle of love, a miracle of kindness, a miracle of God's blessing on the people. It was a sign, they felt, a sign of God's love, a sign of God's care, a sign of God's blessing, a sign that they were a precious part of God's family.

And who was Jesus, they wondered? Was he God's miracle worker come among them, the one from whom God's love would flow freely and generously? The one who would feed them with God's bread? The one who would love them with God's love? The one who would touch them with God's blessings? The one who would lead them to give thanks to God for gifts without number? It was said often in their homes that one day God would bless them in just such a way.

The more the people had these wonderful thoughts about Jesus the more a sort of fever of excitement and enthusiasm for Jesus gripped them. They began to call out the name of Jesus. Jesus! Jesus! They wanted Jesus to be their king. He would put everything in the world right. "Jesus for king," they chanted. They surged forward to declare him king and carry him shoulder high into the city. It was a rich compliment to Jesus from the people. It was their way of blessing him. It was their way of wanting to follow him and give him a place of honor in their lives. But he wasn't after kingship or power or grand things like that. He slipped away from them and went to a quiet place in the mountains to be with God. He stayed there for some time.

Call to Faith

Jesus, you are the one from whom God's love flows freely and generously.

You are the one who feeds us with God's bread.

You are the one who loves us with God's love.

You are the one who touches us with God's blessings.

You are the one who leads us to give thanks to God for gifts without number.

Call to Action

At Mass, this is a day for linking bread with Jesus. We must make much of the offertory procession and the blessing of bread that is the work of human hands. The eucharistic prayer, as always, should be said with careful actions and measured words. The bread becomes the bread of life.

The hymns should follow a bread/bread of life theme.

Eighteenth Sunday in Ordinary Time

Gospel
A reading from the holy Gospel according to John (6:24–35)

So when the crowd saw that neither Jesus nor his disciples were there, they themselves got into the boats and went to Capernaum looking for Jesus.

When they found him on the other side of the sea, they said to him, "Rabbi, when did you come here?" Jesus answered them, "Very truly, I tell you, you are looking for me, not because you saw signs, but because you ate your fill of the loaves. Do not work for the food that perishes, but for the food that endures for eternal life, which the Son of Man will give you. For it is on him that God the Father has set his seal." Then they said to him, "What must we do to perform the works of God?" Jesus answered them, "This is the work of God, that you believe in him whom he has sent." So they said to him, "What sign are you going to give us then, so that we may see it and believe you? What work are you performing? Our ancestors ate the manna in the wilderness; as it is written, 'He gave them bread from heaven to eat.'" Then Jesus said to them, "Very truly, I tell you, it was not Moses who gave you the bread from heaven, but it is my Father who gives you the true bread from heaven. For the bread of God is that which comes down from heaven and gives life to the world." They said to him, "Sir, give us this bread always."

Jesus said to them, "I am the bread of life. Whoever comes to me will never be hungry, and whoever believes in me will never be thirsty."

The gospel of the Lord.

Overview
The bread we eat at Mass is Jesus, the bread of life. It is a tremendous mystery of faith.

Throughout the gospels in this liturgical year, we been given many vivid portraits of Jesus. We hope that the children have come to see Jesus as a real person through his encounters with, for example, the leper, Jairus, Simon's mother-in-law, the disciples in the boat, the disciples in the hollow of the mountain who prayed with him, the disciples who saw him in glory, the five thousand who were hungry, the people who opposed him and wanted to take him down a peg, and his encounters with the devil. They could have quite a portrait of him by now. If they bring this portrait, which is part of their imagination and memory, to Mass and interpret Jesus, the bread of life in the light of what they already know and feel about Jesus, then Jesus, the bread of life will have a richness and a reality for them.

Focusing Experiences

A portrait comes alive when we know the person in the portrait, when we know his or her story, personality, faults, failings, strengths, values.

We are presented with a story of Jesus today: Jesus the bread of life. It would be worthwhile to review the highlights of the story of Jesus for us so far, as experienced by the children.

Exploring the Word of God

In the days that followed it was still a big mystery how Jesus fed five thousand people with five barley loaves and two fishes. No one denied it happened. Some people said it was the work of God, a blessing from God on God's people through the hands of Jesus. Others couldn't get over the wonder of it, had never seen the like before.

Some people followed Jesus on to Capernaum, their minds still filled with the wonder and the mystery of what happened on the shore of the Sea of Galilee. Jesus knew they were thinking of bread multiplied, wonder works, and perhaps more excitement to come. "Yesterday," he said, "the people ate bread on the shore of the Sea of Galilee." They remembered only too well the excitement on that occasion. Now they sensed that the best was yet to come. "I will give you the bread of life." The bread of life? What was this he was saying? Bread that would give life forever? It was an opportunity no one could miss. "Give us this bread of life," they said. He stood before them and said directly and simply, "I am the bread of life." They couldn't get over it. He was the bread of life? Here was a mystery of mysteries. A deeper mystery they couldn't understand. Here he was offering them life, life beyond the grave, life beyond death, life forever. That's what he said.

Only God, they figured, could do that. So what connection did Jesus have with God? That was the big question. Everyone in the crowd seemed to be talking about Jesus on the way home. He was the talk of the land for many days and nights afterwards.

Call to Faith

Jesus, you are the bread of life.

Jesus, friend of Jairus, you are the bread of life.

Jesus, friend of Simon's mother-in-law, you are the bread of life.

Jesus, friend to the disciples especially in the boat when they were about to perish, you are the bread of life.

Jesus, friend to the leper, you are the bread of life.

Jesus, friend to the five thousand hungry people, you are the bread of life.

Jesus, bread of life, come and meet with us today in this celebration.

Call to Action

The title, Jesus, bread of life, might be focused on several times during this Mass.

The songs, hymns, and banners might have the same focus.

Use one of the eucharistic prayers for children, which allows children to celebrate Jesus, the bread of life with a variety of responses.

"This is Jesus, the bread of life," might be an appropriate invitation to communion.

NINETEENTH SUNDAY IN ORDINARY TIME

Gospel
A reading from the holy Gospel according to John (6:41–51)

Then the Jews began to complain about Jesus because he said, "I am the bread that came down from heaven." They were saying, "Is not this Jesus, the son of Joseph, whose father and mother we know? How can he now say, 'I have come down from heaven'?" Jesus answered them, "Do not complain among yourselves. I am the bread of life. Your ancestors ate the manna in the wilderness, and they died. This is the bread that comes down from heaven, so that one may eat of it and not die. I am the living bread that came down from heaven. Whoever eats of this bread will live forever; and the bread that I will give for the life of the world is my flesh."

The gospel of the Lord.

Overview
John's gospel for this Sunday is not a story but a reflection with a eucharistic theme. The homily for children should also be a reflection with a eucharistic theme.

The homily should continue throughout the Mass with eucharistic hymns of worship, a special eucharistic prayer for children, and well chosen words of commentary and prayer to lead the children into a real experience of meeting with Jesus, the bread of life.

Exploring the Word of God
(A reflective dialogue taken from *The Columba Lectionary for Masses with Children*)

Priest	"Body of Christ. Body of Christ."
Onlooker	What did the priest say?
Believer	He said "Body of Christ."
Onlooker	What does that mean?
Believer	As the priest is giving out holy communion, he holds the host before each person to say he is giving the body of Christ.

Onlooker	How can that small piece of bread be the body of Christ?
Believer	It's a miracle.
Onlooker	How do you mean a miracle?
Believer	It is God who makes the bread to be the body of Christ.
Onlooker	Isn't it hard to accept that God makes the bread to be the body of Christ?
Believer	You need to believe, to have faith.
Onlooker	Believe what?
Believer	You need to believe that God loves us a lot. You need to have faith in God's love. You need to believe that God loves us so much that God would give us Jesus to be our Lord and Savior. God gives us the Lord Jesus in holy communion.
Onlooker	Are you saying that it is not bread but Jesus who comes in holy communion?
Believer	Our belief is that Jesus comes to us in holy communion. We meet him in holy communion. It's a precious time for us. In holy communion we meet our Lord.

Call to Faith

Jesus, you are the bread of life.

You feed us with God's love so that we can become faithful sons and daughters of God.

You feed us with your friendship so that we will get to know you better.

You feed us with kindness so that we can show kindness to others.

You feed us with joy so that we can be joyful and make joy for others.

You feed us with concern about others so that we can be generous.

You feed us with love so that we can show love.

You feed us to change our world so that the world can be a better place.

You feed us to change ourselves to be better people, better sons or daughters, better friends, better classmates, better people.

You feed us to overcome the evil that can easily trap us into selfishness or meanness.

We gather round your table at Mass to eat the bread of life, to grow in friendship with you, and to become strong sons and daughters of God.

Twentieth Sunday in Ordinary Time

Gospel
A reading from the holy Gospel according to John (6:51–58)

Jesus said, "I am the living bread that came down from heaven. Whoever eats of this bread will live forever; and the bread that I will give for the life of the world is my flesh."

The Jews then disputed among themselves, saying, "How can this man give us his flesh to eat?" So Jesus said to them, "Very truly, I tell you, unless you eat the flesh of the Son of Man and drink his blood, you have no life in you. Those who eat my flesh and drink my blood have eternal life. Those who eat my flesh and drink my blood abide in me, and I in them. This is the bread that came down from heaven. The one who eats this bread will live forever."

The gospel of the Lord.

Overview
On this Sunday we acknowledge the link between the Last Supper and holy communion. The words of Jesus ring in our ears: "Take and eat, this is my body." "The one who eats this bread will live forever." We highlight the words of Jesus.

Exploring the Word of God
After the reading of the gospel have a group of adults mime the actions of the Last Supper. The twelve sit around a table with their leader. Bread is taken. The words "This is my body" are said. This is followed by "Take and eat." The wheaten bread is broken and shared out among the twelve. The same with the wine.

The final words addressed to the congregation by the leader are: "Do this in memory of me." Each row in the church takes up the chorus, "Do this in memory of him."

At the beginning of the eucharistic prayer the priest says, "We are assembled, to do what we are now doing, in memory of him."

At the invitation to communion the priest says:
This is the bread of life.
This is the risen Jesus.
This is Jesus our friend.
This is Jesus who brings God's love.
This is Jesus who brings us God's forgiveness.
This is Jesus who asks us to spread love.
This is Jesus who asks us to build a better world.
Happy and blessed are those who are called to his supper.

Twenty-First Sunday in Ordinary Time

Gospel
A reading from the holy Gospel according to John (6:60–69)

When many of his disciples heard it, they said, "This teaching is difficult; who can accept it?" But Jesus, being aware that his disciples were complaining about it, said to them, "Does this offend you? Then what if you were to see the Son of Man ascending to where he was before? It is the spirit that gives life; the flesh is useless. The words that I have spoken to you are spirit and life. But among you there are some who do not believe." So Jesus asked the twelve, "Do you also wish to go away?" Simon Peter answered him, "Lord, to whom can we go? You have the words of eternal life. We have come to believe and know that you are the Holy One of God."

The gospel of the Lord.

Overview
Jesus is the bread of life. What he is saying is hidden, mysterious. It can only be seen with the heart. It can only be grasped with faith. Some see and accept him and follow him. Some do not see and reject him and do not follow him. For those who follow he is the Holy One of God, the only way, the only truth, the only life.

Focusing Experiences
The homily takes the form of a liturgical dance performed by young people in their teens.
   It has several elements:
   The Cross
   The Last Supper
   The Mass

The Cross
The dancers fete Jesus on the cross, which symbolizes the love of Jesus and the sacrifice of love he offered on the cross. This is at the cen-

ter of the first movement. The cross is finally carried on high and placed in a position of honor.

The Last Supper

At the heart of the Last Supper is the phrase over the bread, "This is my body." "I am the bread of life" also has links with the Last Supper. It is the test for all the followers of Jesus. Some accept and believe and dance joyfully with Jesus. Some cannot accept it; they reject what he says, go away dejectedly, and do not dance anymore with Jesus. The disciples, led by Simon Peter, dance wholeheartedly with him, whom they recognize as the Holy One of God.

The Mass

The dancers are present at Mass. They share in and eat the bread of life and dance into everyday life, one wearing overalls, one wearing a white coat, one carrying a briefcase, one carrying a satchel of books. They dance with Jesus and make him welcome in their world.

Exploring the Word of God

They were there talking in small groups. They believed in Jesus. They wanted to follow him. He seemed to offer a good way. What he said made sense. But this last thing, "I am the bread of life," made no sense. What did it mean? How could Jesus be bread for people? After much soul searching some of these turned and walked away. It was too much for them.

The disciples were different. Simon Peter spoke the mind of all. He said very simply, "We believe. We know you have the words of eternal life. We know you are the Holy One of God."

Call to Faith

Jesus is the bread of life.
   bread to grow in love
   bread to grow in forgiveness
   bread to grow in joy
   bread to grow in peace
   bread for the struggle to overcome selfishness
   bread for the struggle to overcome meanness
   bread for the journey of faith with Jesus

Call to Action

The eucharistic theme will be supported by dance (homily) and by song (for the rest of the Mass). The acclamations of the eucharistic prayer for children will be especially significant.

Twenty-Second Sunday
in Ordinary Time

Gospel
A reading from the holy Gospel according to Mark (7:1–8,14–15,21–23)

Now when the Pharisees and some of the scribes who had come from Jerusalem gathered around him, they noticed that some of his disciples were eating with defiled hands, that is, without washing them. (For the Pharisees, and all the Jews, do not eat unless they thoroughly wash their hands, thus observing the tradition of the elders; and they do not eat anything from the market unless they wash it; and there are also many other traditions that they observe, the washing of cups, pots, and bronze kettles.) So the Pharisees and the scribes asked him, "Why do your disciples not live according to the tradition of the elders, but eat with defiled hands?" He said to them, "Isaiah prophesied rightly about you hypocrites, as it is written,

'This people honors me with
their lips,
but their hearts are far from
me;
in vain do they worship me,
teaching human precepts as
doctrines.'
You abandon the commandment of God and hold to human tradition."

The gospel of the Lord.

Overview
One doesn't want to show disrespect to people who observe religious traditions with great fervor. But neither can we let ourselves be locked into traditions that are given an importance they don't really have.

Jesus is making a point about priorities in today's story. The followers of Jesus will not be judged on the meticulous way customs are carried out but on the way they love God and the way they love their neighbor.

Our role with the children is not to downgrade customs but to highlight the core value of Christianity, which is loving in all its forms.

Is it easy enough to speak about the importance of love but it will be better to ask someone, such as a parent, health worker, or therapist, to give testimony about the importance of loving. When you do that you are really making the teaching or homily do its work.

Focusing Experiences

Think of some customs that we follow, such as a handshake or a wave goodbye.

Could you imagine it being a sin if you didn't shake someone's hand when you meet? Or if you didn't bless yourself when you go into church?

Exploring the Word of God

It seemed a small thing. Jesus' disciples didn't bathe their hands in water before eating. This was noticed by the officials, who were quick to complain. They said Jesus' disciples were out of line. They were breaking with tradition. They wouldn't be right with God if they didn't bathe their hands the way it had always been done. It was the custom, and customs had to be kept. If they weren't kept what would the world come to? Worse still, it was flying in the face of God to put aside these customs.

Jesus saw things differently. He felt these experts were making the customs sound like the Ten Commandments of God. Jesus was quick to point out that keeping customs isn't enough to keep you right with God. Observing customs is an outside thing, he said, but goodness comes from inside, from the head and from the heart.

Washing your hands won't keep you right with God, he said. What will keep you right with God is love. You have to love God and love your neighbor.

People who were listening thought what Jesus said made a lot of sense. Loving was something that took a real effort—like loving your enemy or loving someone who has done you a bad turn or loving someone who is a stranger or an outcast. It wasn't easy to be loving. It took commitment.

The experts weren't pleased when they were told that loving is about more than bathing your hands. Jesus left them in no doubt that love comes before anything else.

Call to Faith

We are called to show love.

We are called to become loving people.

We are called to become people for whom loving is natural.

Call to Action

If loving is a priority then we have to have some focus on this essential Christian activity.

Have a parent give some kind of testimony to the importance of love.

Have a health or social worker give testimony to the importance of love as a healer for people who are hurt.

The Mass should resound to the sound of songs with the theme of love.

Could we all pray to be more loving?

Twenty-Third Sunday
in Ordinary Time

Gospel
A reading from the holy Gospel according to Mark (7:31–37)

Then he returned from the region of Tyre, and went by way of Sidon towards the Sea of Galilee, in the region of the Decapolis. They brought to him a deaf man who had an impediment in his speech; and they begged him to lay his hand on him. He took him aside in private, away from the crowd, and put his fingers into his ears, and he spat and touched his tongue. Then looking up to heaven, he sighed and said to him, "Ephphatha," that is, "Be opened." And immediately his ears were opened, his tongue was released, and he spoke plainly. Then Jesus ordered them to tell no one; but the more he ordered them, the more zealously they proclaimed it. They were astounded beyond measure, saying, "He has done everything well; he even makes the deaf to hear and the mute to speak."

The gospel of the Lord.

Overview
The gospel story for today is about Jesus curing a deaf man who also has a speech impediment. As with all the stories in the gospels, we will be pleased if the children inhabit the story at a basic level. It's the right beginning. The nuances will come later. It means they get to know Jesus as a person, as a healer, as someone who cares. They are on the road of friendship with Jesus.

There is another strand in the story that we will develop in the Call to Faith: We too need the cure of Jesus to speak and hear in a way that is loving and caring.

Focusing Experiences
Think about:

Listening and not hearing—that's passive listening. Active listening is listening and hearing.

We can listen but we don't really hear the other person's concerns. We don't show any interest. We don't ask any exploratory questions.

We don't follow up on what we are being told. We don't inquire. We can listen with our ears, but we also have to listen with our hearts.

Exploring the Word of God

He was quite deaf, this man from Decapolis. And he had a bad problem with his speech. They brought him to Jesus for a cure. Jesus took him aside from the crowd where he and the man were in private.

He laid his hands on the man's ears. He put spittle on the man's tongue. Then Jesus looked up to heaven and said "Ephphatha" which means, "be opened." And whatever had held the man back from hearing and speaking was gone. He was able to speak. The man who once was deaf went back to the people who brought him to Jesus, and they couldn't get over his hearing and his speech. They tried all kinds of tricks on him, whispering and shouting, pretending to speak and miming. It was all the same. He could hear and speak perfectly.

Everyone heard the news that Jesus had cured the man's deafness and got rid of his speech impediment. They were all talking about it. Some people saw it as wonder works. Others saw it as God's work through the hands of Jesus. It was a sign, they said, of the new age that God had promised.

Call to Faith

Jesus, you touch our ears because you want us to hear the Word of God and put it into action.

Jesus, you touch our lips because you want us to speak with strength and courage. You want us to show that we care. Sometimes we fail.

Jesus, you touch our ears because you want us to hear the cries of our friends who are lonely or upset. We don't always hear. We don't always want to hear. We want to be a little deaf. It's not always easy to listen and to unblock whatever is stopping us from hearing.

Jesus, you touch our ears because you want us to hear our parents. We sometimes play deaf. We sometimes ignore them. Unblock our hearts because we first have to hear them with our hearts.

Jesus, touch our ears again today that we may hear the call of God in our hearts.

Jesus, touch our lips again today that we may speak with love.

Call to Action

Ask each child to listen again to some request that has been ignored—a request from a friend, a teacher, a parent. Listen again and respond! Take the necessary action. Encourage them to listen as Jesus wants them to listen.

Have someone give a brief talk on what it means to be a good listener.

Thank God for the gift of speech by celebrating with a song of joy.

Twenty-Fourth Sunday
in Ordinary Time

Gospel
A reading from the holy Gospel according to Mark (8:27–35)

Jesus went on with his disciples to the village of Caesarea Philippi; and on the way he asked his disciples, "Who do people say that I am?" And they answered him, "John the Baptist; and others, Elijah; and still others, one of the prophets." He asked them, "But who do you say that I am?" Peter answered him, "You are the Messiah."

The gospel of the Lord.

Overview
Peter makes his profession of faith.

We can celebrate our belief in Jesus too. If we can find someone who is ready to declare faith in Jesus before the children and say what difference Jesus makes to their life, it will add a valuable new dimension to the teaching or homily.

Exploring the Word of God
In those days everybody was wondering who Jesus was. Some people said he was John the Baptist come back to life. Some others said he was the famous prophet Elijah. Some people said he was this or that prophet. Everything he did and everything he said had the ring and the hallmark of God about it. He had a strong connection with God. That was clear. But was that all?

Jesus asked Peter what he thought. Peter had already made up his mind. Peter said, "You're the Messiah of God. I know it." Saying he was the Messiah was saying plenty. It was saying everything. It was saying that Jesus was the promised one. It was saying that Jesus was God in the flesh. It was a very big thing to say. There was nothing more to be said. Peter was saying what no one had ever said so openly and so clearly. Peter was declaring his faith in Jesus.

Call to Faith

Jesus, you are the Messiah.
> You are the promised one of God.
> You are the Anointed One.
> You are the Christ.
> You are the Son of the Living God.
> You are the Beloved Son.
> You are the risen Christ.
> You are the Savior.
> You are our leader.
> You are our friend.
> You are our brother.
> You are our Shepherd.
> You are our King.

Call to Action

Ask someone in the parish to give a witness statement to the children by saying what it means to have faith in Jesus.

Home, school, church ties always need to be strengthened. It might be a time to take a poll of parents to find out their needs.

Twenty-Fifth Sunday
in Ordinary Time

Gospel
A reading from the holy Gospel according to Mark (9:30–37)

They went on from there and passed through Galilee. He did not want anyone to know it; for he was teaching his disciples, saying to them, "The Son of Man is to be betrayed into human hands, and they will kill him, and three days after being killed, he will rise again." But they did not understand what he was saying and were afraid to ask him.

Then they came to Capernaum; and when he was in the house he asked them, "What were you arguing about on the way?" But they were silent, for on the way they had argued with one another who was the greatest. He sat down, called the twelve, and said to them, "Whoever wants to be first must be last of all and servant of all." Then he took a little child and put it among them; and taking it in his arms, he said to them, "Whoever welcomes one such child in my name welcomes me, and whoever welcomes me welcomes not me but the one who sent me."

The gospel of the Lord.

Overview
There are various strands to this gospel.

Following Jesus will lead not to kingship but to the cross. That's a shock for the disciples who had high hopes of future success, honor, and good positions to match.

What is of particular interest to us is that Jesus presents a mother's love as a model for the selflessness that is at the heart of real Christian living. The children know only too well how selfless a mother's love is. It is a wonderful image on which to build a homily for children.

Focusing Experiences
Think about:

A mother's love. Use examples from the children about a mother's love. Do a survey in advance.

There is a saying: "A mother's love is a blessing." What does that mean?

Exploring the Word of God

There was Jesus hinting to the disciples about a future full of trouble, full of suffering, full of pain, maybe even death. They didn't seem to understand what was in his mind. They imagined a future full of promise, full of success. God was on their side—what did they have to worry about? They couldn't really take in what Jesus was saying. They kept on thinking about a bright future, and they saw themselves being appointed to important roles as leaders in God's new kingdom. Which of them would be chief? Who would be assistant chief? They all wanted to be important people in the future. And they began to argue about their roles in the new kingdom of God.

Jesus heard them arguing and gathered them around for a heart to heart talk about all this. "There will be no important roles in the future," he said. There will be no chiefs and no assistant chiefs. In God's kingdom there are no chiefs, only servants. In God's kingdom there are no leaders, only helpers."

Then he took a little child who was standing there near him with her mother. He put his arms around the child. "That's what you have to do," he said. "Be like a mother. Be caring. Be protective. Be loving. Put yourselves not first but second as mothers do. Be generous. Be unselfish."

The disciples were taken aback by all this but they understood what Jesus was asking of them.

Call to Faith

We are called to be loving like mothers.

We are called to be forgiving like mothers.

We are called to generous like mothers.

We are called to be tender when others are wounded or upset.

We are called to be strong when others are feeling down.

We are called to be protective when others are feeling weak or vulnerable.

We are called to remember when others forget.

We are called to be full of heart, like mothers are.

Call to Action

Ask a mother to say how a mother is called to be everything to everybody—care-giver, chef, servant, friend, protector, adviser. Jesus chose the image well!

Let the mother's talk be part of the homily.

Twenty-Sixth Sunday in Ordinary Time

Gospel
A reading from the holy Gospel according to Mark (9:38–43, 45, 47–48)

John said to him, "Teacher, we saw someone casting out demons in your name, and we tried to stop him, because he was not following us." But Jesus said, "Do not stop him; for no one who does a deed of power in my name will be able soon afterward to speak evil of me. Whoever is not against us is for us. For truly I tell you, whoever gives you a cup of water to drink because you bear the name of Christ will by no means lose the reward.

"If any of you put a stumbling block before one of these little ones who believe in me, it would be better for you if a great millstone were hung around your neck and you were thrown into the sea. If your hand causes you to stumble, cut it off; it is better for you to enter life maimed than to have two hands and to go to hell, to the unquenchable fire. And if your foot causes you to stumble, cut it off; it is better for you to enter life lame than to have two feet and to be thrown into hell. And if your eye causes you to stumble, tear it out; it is better for you to enter the kingdom of God with one eye than to have two eyes and to be thrown into hell."

The gospel of the Lord.

Overview
In today's gospel Jesus speaks with passion and poetry. We shouldn't be afraid of his poetic exaggerations. It is strong and salutary advice. The children will be able to cope with and hear the message. It is a genre they are well used to.

Focusing Experiences
In our language we sometimes exaggerate to underline a point. It's a way of speaking. Think of the outrageous things we say to make a point:

I almost died!
I could kill you!
You are dead when you get home!
My mother hit the roof!

Exploring the Word of God

In the days of Jesus preachers often exaggerated to make a point. It was a way of talking that people understood.

Jesus held up his hand. If this hand works against God it is useless. It is dead. If this hand hurts other people it is a crying shame. If this hand makes trouble for God or God's people it is better to cut it off and throw it into the rubbish dump.

He pointed to his eye. If this eye looks on God's world without love it is useless. If this eye looks at people without any concern it is dead. If this eye causes hurt to other people it deserves to be plucked out and thrown into the rubbish dump.

He pointed to his foot. If this foot works against God it is useless. It is dead. If this foot works against God it is better to cut it off and throw it into the rubbish dump.

Call to Faith

Hands are for waving and greeting.
Hands are for reaching out and touching.
Hands are for supporting and comforting.
Hands are for caressing and loving.
Hands are for forgiving and making up.
Hands are for working and making.
Hands are for clapping with joy.

Jesus needs our hands.
It is hands that can steal.
It is hands that can hurt.
It is hands that refuse a welcome.
Such hands are cold and are useless to Jesus.
Jesus needs our hands to make the world a better place.

Jesus needs our feet.
Feet are for walking in company with others.
Feet are for walking away from trouble.
Feet are for walking in procession.
It is feet that walk us into trouble.
It is feet that refuse to help.
It is feet that are lazy when our help is needed.

Such feet are useless to Jesus.
Jesus needs our feet to make the world a better place.

Jesus needs our eyes.
Eyes are for looking at the beauty of God's world.
Eyes are for welcoming.
Eyes are for seeing what has to be done.
But eyes can hurt.
Eyes can ignore.
Eyes can pierce.
Such eyes are useless to Jesus.
Jesus needs our eyes to make the world a better place.

Call to Action

This is an ideal time for mime or liturgical dance that involves hands, eyes, and feet.

Sing songs that emphasize our obligations to all our sisters and brothers.

TWENTY-SEVENTH SUNDAY IN ORDINARY TIME

Gospel
A reading from the holy Gospel according to Mark (10:2–16)

People were bringing little children to him in order that he might touch them; and the disciples spoke sternly to them. But when Jesus saw this, he was indignant and said to them, "Let the little children come to me; do not stop them; for it is to such as these that the kingdom of God belongs. Truly I tell you, whoever does not receive the kingdom of God as a little child will never enter it." And he took them up in his arms, laid his hands on them, and blessed them.

The gospel of the Lord.

Overview
Homilies take various forms. Today's gospel reading is rather special. Jesus blesses the children. It is their moment of glory. Both our teaching about this gospel and the homily should reflect the importance this reading has for children because it says in a beautiful and tender way that Jesus really does love children.

Focusing Experiences
Think about:
relationships with adults. Who are the key adults in children's lives? (include pop stars, sports heroes, etc.)
What do we want from adults who are close to us? security...love...a hearing...(list them)

Exploring the Word of God
(Our teaching or homily might take the form of a group of children miming the action of Jesus blessing the children while other children or adults reading the following supporting script [from *The Columba Lectionary for Masses with Children*] over the microphones.)

Narrator   God's gift of love is there for children too. They get God's gift of love from parents, from friends, from brothers and sisters. Jesus shared God's gift of love with children who came along with their parents to meet them.

Interviewer	I believe there was a very large crowd of people around Jesus?
Child 1	A very large crowd was all around Jesus. Everyone was standing and stretching to hear what was going on. The crowd kept getting bigger and bigger. We children were told to stand back. We were told that what Jesus was saying had nothing to do with us.
Child 2	My mother said it did have something to do with us. She said she wanted Jesus to bless us.
Child 1	A big man said, "No more blessings today. Jesus is worn out. He needs to rest. Children are not allowed around here. They'll have to move on."
Child 3	But we didn't go away.
Child 1	Jesus came through the crowd and told the man who was sending us away to take it easy. Jesus said he wanted to bless the children.
Child 2	We stood there very still and very pleased. Jesus blessed every single one of us with God's blessing.
Interviewer	How did the blessing feel?
Child 3	It felt great because Jesus is God's prophet!
Child 2	My mother said you could tell by his actions that Jesus really loved children.

Call to Faith

Jesus, you bless us.
Jesus, you love us.
Jesus, you are our friend.
We are your friends too.
We love you.
We honor you.
We thank and praise God for you.

Call to Action

Sing songs of Jesus and the children.

Have a special blessing for the children at the end of Mass and a special invitation to go out and show love.

TWENTY-EIGHTH SUNDAY IN ORDINARY TIME

Gospel
A reading from the holy Gospel according to Mark (10:17–30)

As Jesus was setting out on a journey, a man ran up and knelt before him, and asked him, "Good Teacher, what must I do to inherit eternal life?" Jesus said to him, "Why do you call me good? No one is good but God alone. You know the commandments: 'You shall not murder; You shall not commit adultery; You shall not steal; You shall not bear false witness; You shall not defraud; Honor your father and mother.'" He said to him, "Teacher, I have kept all these since my youth." Jesus, looking at him, loved him and said, "You lack one thing; go, sell what you own, and give the money to the poor, and you will have treasure in heaven; then come, follow me." When he heard this, he was shocked and went away grieving, for he had many possessions.

The gospel of the Lord.

Overview
Today's story is all about values. What are the priorities in my life? What are the really significant attachments? Are some of these attachments positive, some negative? How do I respond to the values that Jesus is proclaiming?

Children need help and encouragement to be generous and to develop an attitude of generosity. They need to get a lead from us. Today's story and the actions that flow from it will point them in the right direction.

Focusing Experiences
What are our favorite attachments?
  video games?
  TV?
  being with friends?
  clothes?

gadgets?
books?
animals?
eating?
music?

Exploring the Word of God

This man came up to Jesus. "I think I am doing everything right," he said. "I keep the commandments. All of them. I don't miss out on a single one. I don't cheat and I don't lie and I don't play false with my neighbor. What should I do, therefore, to become your disciple?" The man was very wealthy and Jesus sensed he was attached to his money.

Jesus was right. Money meant everything to the man. He loved his money. It was his most precious possession. He couldn't imagine life without his money and all the little comforts that it brought.

"If you want to be my disciple," Jesus said, "go and sell what you have and give it to the poor." It was like stabbing the man in the heart. You could see the pain in his face. Anything but parting with his money! His money was everything to him. It was more important than love, more important than happiness. If only Jesus had mentioned something difficult, something *really* difficult—but not that! He would try anything, but to ask him to be parted from his money? That was impossible. The man didn't even look at Jesus or give him an answer. He kept his head down and went back down the road the way he came.

Call to Faith

We get attached to toys.

We get attached to books.

We get attached to pocket money.

We get attached to being the center of attention in the family.

We get attached to friends.

Jesus calls us to loosen our attachments and be ready to follow new or different paths.

Call to Action

Arrange to have a toy sale or a book sale for a worthy cause. Some children store away toys or books they have outgrown. It is good to share. This might be an opportunity to loosen an attachment in the cause of spreading love.

Twenty-Ninth Sunday
in Ordinary Time

Gospel
A reading from the holy Gospel according to Mark (10:35–45)

James and John, the sons of Zebedee, came forward to Jesus and said to him, "Teacher, we want you to do for us whatever we ask of you." And he said to them, "What is it you want me to do for you?" And they said to him, "Grant us to sit, one at your right hand and one at your left, in your glory." But Jesus said to them, "You do not know what you are asking. Are you able to drink the cup that I drink, or be baptized with the baptism that I am baptized with?" They replied, "We are able." Then Jesus said to them, "The cup that I drink you will drink; and with the baptism with which I am baptized, you will be baptized; but to sit at my right hand or at my left is not mine to grant, but it is for those for whom it has been prepared."

When the ten heard this, they began to be angry with James and John. So Jesus called them and said to them, "You know that among the Gentiles those whom they recognize as their rulers lord it over them, and their great ones are tyrants over them. But it is not so among you; but whoever wishes to become great among you must be your servant, and whoever wishes to be first among you must be slave of all. For the Son of Man came not to be served but to serve, and to give his life a ransom for many."

The gospel of the Lord.

Overview
The Christian call to service is very serious—no fudging, no half measures. It is a call to service. Period. It is the core value. We have to look out for the needs of other people. We have to reach out. James and John thought they could work at it from the top. That isn't Jesus' way.

Focusing Experiences
The teacher or homilist could begin with a tongue-in-cheek advertise-

ment for a helper in a family in the parish, profiling the ideal candidate, and giving a job description. It is, of course, a mirror image of the children in their "called" role to service in the Christian community!

Exploring the Word of God
Two brothers, James and John, the sons of Zebedee, asked to have a quiet word with Jesus. He took them out of earshot of the rest of the disciples and invited them to speak out their minds."Well, it's like this," they said. "We have followed you from the beginning. We have done our best to be good disciples. We've held nothing back."

"I agree with that," said Jesus. "I couldn't have asked for more."

"Well, the point is this," said the disciples, "when you come into your kingdom, when you rule over the whole world in God's name, you will remember us, won't you? We were thinking you might give us a special place—at the top. Can we be your leaders? You will need some trusted friends to head up the organization—people you can trust to take charge of things. Can we be your number one and your number two? You know what we mean: leaders. Your leaders. You won't regret it! We'll do a good job as your right hand men.

"We hope you don't mind us speaking up like this. We are just, sort of, putting our names down now for something worthwhile in the future."

"Do you really know what you are getting into?" asked Jesus. "Do you know what you are asking for? Do you know what you are facing?"

"Of course, we know," they said. "We'll be able to handle it. We could handle anything. We're not afraid."

They didn't know. They hadn't a clue. They were very wide of the mark. What was on Jesus' mind was different from what they were thinking. Jesus didn't see a future of kingdoms and glory, power and palaces, and top jobs for his friends. He saw a future where he would face opposition—people spitting on him, people turning against him, being dragged into court, suffering, maybe even death at the end of it all.

James and John saw honor and glory, and the crowds cheering Jesus on, people honoring him. They saw a court but it wasn't a law court with prison cells underneath, but a royal court with royal music and rooms full of servants and all the trappings and comforts that rulers have. As James and John saw it, the disciples were to be part of the excitement, part of the honor, part of the leadership in the new kingdom of God. And they would have the most important jobs—if only Jesus agreed.

Some of the other disciples couldn't help but overhear what James and John were asking, and they weren't a bit pleased. To be honest they were quite unhappy about it. The annoyance showed in their faces. They raised their voices in protest. They felt James and John were out of order. They complained to each other that the two sons of Zebedee had no right to be setting themselves up like this.

What place were they themselves going to have in the future? Were they to be forgotten? Were they going to end up as servants to James and John?

Jesus heard it all. He beckoned to them to gather around him.

"Listen," he said, "you can either think of kings or servants. Kings have everything. Servants have nothing. Kings give commands and they are obeyed. Servants don't give commands. Kings and the like speak down to people. Servants speak from the heart but they have no authority to command. Kings have people around them to honor them. Servants have no one around them to honor them. I am not like a king. I am like a servant. That is the will of God. That is the choice I have made. Those who want to be like kings and lords can go and live in palaces. It's not for me. It's not for those who follow me. It's not for you.

"I want to serve, not to be a boss. I want to be with the poor, not with the great and mighty. I want to be a helper to people, not a ruler over them. You and I are not heading for palaces. We face something quite different. Have no doubt about that."

Call to Faith

Our families sometimes need our time, our attention, our energy, our love.

They need our help.

Our brothers and sisters sometimes need our time, our attention, our energy, our love.

They need our help.

Our schoolmates need our help.

Our teacher needs our help.

Our priest needs our help.

We are called to help.

We are called to serve like Jesus.

Call to Action

Spread slogans like "Called to Serve," "Help needed," "Jesus says service is the thing" around the church.

Sing songs that reflect the theme, "Called to Serve."

Repeat the call to serve in different ways throughout the liturgy.

Ask a teenaged member of some voluntary organization to speak to the children about the importance of service to ourselves and to the community.

THIRTIETH SUNDAY IN ORDINARY TIME

Gospel
A reading from the holy Gospel according to Mark (10:46–52)

As Jesus and his disciples and a large crowd were leaving Jericho, Bartimaeus son of Timaeus, a blind beggar, was sitting by the roadside. When he heard that it was Jesus of Nazareth, he began to shout out and say, "Jesus, Son of David, have mercy on me!" Many sternly ordered him to be quiet, but he cried out even more loudly, "Son of David, have mercy on me!" Jesus stood still and said, "Call him here." And they called the blind man, saying to him, "Take heart; get up, he is calling you." So throwing off his cloak, he sprang up and came to Jesus. Then Jesus said to him, "What do you want me to do for you?" The blind man said to him, "My teacher, let me see again." Jesus said to him, "Go; your faith has made you well." Immediately he regained his sight and followed him on the way.

The gospel of the Lord.

Overview
Jesus is recognized as the Messiah by Bartimaeus the blind beggar. Bartimaeus was on the edge of society, a bit of an outcast like all beggars. But Jesus makes him the hero of this story. His prayer is exemplary. He doesn't give in. He keeps asking. He won't be shouted down by anyone. His faith in Jesus is also exemplary. He believes with a fierce passion. He becomes a follower.

On this day we introduce the children to Bartimaeus the man of prayer, the man of faith, the man who followed Jesus.

Focusing Experiences
Perseverance is a concept worth exploring today:
in sport
in study
in work
in hobbies
in friendship
in love

Exploring the Word of God

There was a large crowd on the road from Jericho to Jerusalem. It was pilgrimage time, and the road was crowded with pilgrims. Jesus and his disciples were among the crowd. People recognized Jesus, and a ripple of excitement spread through the crowd with the news that Jesus was among them. Pilgrims nudged each other when they caught a glimpse of him or told their friends a story they knew about this good and holy man.

A blind man sat by the roadside begging from the pilgrims who passed. He was quick to pick up that Jesus was in the crowd. He had been on the lookout for Jesus for a long time. He had heard the stories—every last one of them. He knew Jesus better than most. He had made it his business to ask questions, to inquire, to compare. He was a glutton for information about Jesus. He never, ever missed an opportunity to ask about Jesus. Every scrap of information he heard about Jesus he remembered and stored in his mind. Gradually, over many months, he came to a conclusion. The information all fitted together. He figured out that Jesus was God's Messiah. He was convinced that Jesus had been sent by God. It was clear that Jesus was God's voice for the people. He was determined, if he got a chance, to honor Jesus.

When he heard that Jesus was in the crowd coming toward him he began to shout out, "Jesus, Son of David, have pity on me!" "Son of David" was a special title, given only to the Messiah. People were shocked to hear Jesus openly named as the Messiah. They had their own ideas about Jesus. It did cross their minds that Jesus might be the Messiah, but to hear it shouted out by a blind man sitting in the dust at the side of the road begging for food and small coins didn't seem right. It was the kind of big news that they expected might come from the high priest in the temple at Jerusalem. They were embarrassed at the shouting and the pronouncements of the blind man. So they tried to keep him quiet. The news could hardly be true if it was just coming from a beggar. They tried to smother what he was saying with shouts and prayers and raised voices. Some people standing near the beggar appealed to him to lower his voice. "It's upsetting the pilgrims," they said. "It's spoiling the atmosphere." But blind Bartimaeus shouted all the louder. "Jesus, Son of David, have pity on me."

His voice filled a whole stretch of road, and Jesus, who was quite a distance away, heard him clearly. The people near Bartimaeus passed on the message that Jesus wanted to see him. At this good news he jumped up, threw away the beggar's cloak and beggar's bowl, and, with one man on each side of him to guide him, he almost ran in his hurry to meet Jesus.

"How do you want me to help you?" asked Jesus.

"Man of God," said the blind man to him, "let me see again."

Jesus said to him, "Your faith in God has made all the difference." Immediately his sight returned. Bartimaeus became a follower of Jesus and took his place on the road with those who were walking with Jesus to Jerusalem.

Call to Faith

We are called to recognize Jesus as the voice of God for us just as Bartimaeus recognized him and had faith in him.

We are called to pray with the determination that Bartimaeus had.

We are called to ask Jesus to open our eyes to a million and one new ways of showing love.

We are called to follow Jesus with the kind of enthusiasm that Bartimaeus had.

Call to Action

The theme of the Mass could be, "Open our eyes, Lord Jesus." The theme should be referred to in introductions, prayers, and commentary.

A prayer service with the theme of service might be arranged for school or parish church.

Thirty-First Sunday
in Ordinary Time

Gospel
A reading from the holy Gospel according to Mark (12:28–34)

One of the scribes came near and asked Jesus, "Which commandment is the first of all?" Jesus answered, "The first is, 'Hear, O Israel: the Lord our God, the Lord is one; you shall love the Lord your God with all your heart, and with all your soul, and with all your mind, and with all your strength.' The second is this, 'You shall love your neighbor as yourself.' There is no other commandment greater than these."

The gospel of the Lord.

Overview
The importance Jesus gave to showing love as the most pivotal expression of religion did take his contemporaries by surprise. In their list of religious commitments, showing love had its place, high on the list certainly, but not preeminent. With Jesus loving God and neighbor was everything.

We have to lead the children to appreciate that showing love is the challenge we must not shrink from.

Focusing Experiences
Think about love in all its forms, especially in the setting of the home:

Love as love—the affectionate touch, the kiss, the embrace;

Love as care—care for the baby, for the young child, for the older child, for the adolescent;

Love as concern—rules of conduct, warnings, advice, counseling, discipline, sanctions;

Love as commitment—never giving up, never feeling quite finished.

Exploring the Word of God
In the days of Jesus people said that obeying the laws of their great leader Moses was the most important thing God wanted them to do. It was agreed that the next most important thing that God wanted them to do was to worship God by offering sacrifices. It was said that the

third most important thing to do was to show love for their neighbor.

Jesus was asked the question by a scholar, "What do you think is the most important thing God wants us to do? What is your opinion?"

Jesus said, "To love is the first most important thing, and to love is the second most important thing."

People were quite surprised to hear that love was the most important, the highest on the list.

Jesus said, "You must love God with power, with energy, with commitment. And you must love your neighbor as one of your own flesh and blood."

They way he said it made them think. No one had ever put it like that before.

Call to Faith
We are called to love.

We are called to express love at home and at school in a thousand little ways.

We are called to be people who show love in what they say and do.

Call to Action
Ask someone who has experienced God's love in a particular way to give a brief testimony to the children.

The sign of peace at Mass might be extended to include a mime or dance focusing on the theme of love.

Sing songs and hymns of love.

Take special care to emphasize theme of "love one another" in the various parts of this Mass.

THIRTY-SECOND SUNDAY
IN ORDINARY TIME

Gospel
A reading from the holy Gospel according to Mark (12:38–44)

Jesus sat down opposite the treasury, and watched the crowd putting money into the treasury. Many rich people put in large sums. A poor widow came and put in two small copper coins, which are worth a penny. Then he called his disciples and said to them, "Truly I tell you, this poor widow has put in more than all those who are contributing to the treasury. For all of them have contributed out of their abundance; but she out of her poverty has put in everything she had, all she had to live on."

The gospel of the Lord.

Overview

The message from Jesus is clear! Shadow and substance are quite different things. The disciples were impressed with the shadow—the city, its fine buildings, its robed scholars, its men of prayer in prayer shawls drawing approving glances from the crowd. Even the action of the widow who gives her last coin on earth to the upkeep of the temple needs to be probed. It was a reckless kind of generosity that people in authority approved of, but which left this most generous widow penniless and in desolation. She was being exploited.

The disciples were very taken in by all the glitter.

The substance was harder to spot. For those who had eyes to see, the substance was there in the widow woman who gave two pitiful coins for the upkeep of the temple. Her integrity was transparent, her sincerity obvious, her love for God very sure.

In the light of the gospel, adults need to be alerted that the "system" can easily become part of the shadow. We begin to feel at home with the externals.

When we address the children the story of the glitter that impressed the disciples will have its own warning. With them it's worth lingering with the widow. We want to help the children to see that love has little enough to do with scale. Big does not always mean beautiful with God. God looks at the motive. God looks into our hearts.

Children are only slowly climbing the ladder of morality from doing something good to please us (for show) to doing something good because it is worth doing. We have to encourage this growth in moral thinking.

It might appear to children that they can do little enough. Their generosity is limited by circumstances. But look at the widow. Her effort was small but it was her best effort done with heart and generosity. She won praise from Jesus and blessings from God. Children are not powerless before God. It is often the thought that counts.

Focusing Experiences
What does this statement "It is the thought that counts" mean?

Why is a homemade birthday card often much appreciated by your parents on their birthdays?

Why is the small word "sorry," spoken sincerely, often much appreciated?

Exploring the Word of God
The disciples arrived in the great city of Jerusalem with Jesus. It was a time of pilgrimage and pilgrims from every part of the world filled the city. There were crowds everywhere. The disciples were impressed with everything they saw—the crowds, the fine buildings, the shrines, and the temple itself. They were impressed with the men who wore the prayer shawls. Such holy men! Such friends with God! What powerful prayers they must have! They noticed that the men with the prayer shawls were given much respect by the people. And the men in the shawls enjoyed their place in society. Sure, it was only their due.

And the disciples were impressed with the holy scholars in the long robes who carried a rolled-up parchment of the holy Book under their arm. It was obvious they were held in great honor by the people. They seemed to enjoy their popularity and they charged for a consultation about the great Book.

And the disciples were impressed when they came to the treasury at the temple. This was where the donations for the upkeep of the temple were given. People who came from far away were pleased to leave some money for candles, or to help the poor, or just to be remembered in the prayers said in the temple every day. There were thirteen great metal chests. People dropped their coins into a funnel on the lid of the chest and you could hear the echo of your donation as it rattled its way in among the other donations. Wealthy merchants and the like were dropping in gold coins. Everyone saw them and everyone admired what they were doing. The disciples of Jesus saw the glint of the gold and heard the heavy fall of the gold coins. They were terribly impressed with the generosity of these wealthy people.

Others lined up to drop in silver coins. Not as impressive as the gold but impressive all the same. The disciples looked at those who gave large donations with wide-eyed admiration.

Jesus drew their attention to an old lady who was putting in two coins. Not gold, not silver. Very ordinary coins. Everyone had them. They were the kind you bought bread with. She put in the coins. They didn't make much of a rattle, and no one could be too impressed. It was a very small donation.

Jesus could see how the disciples' minds were working and he shared his thoughts with them. Don't be impressed with men who wear showy prayer shawls. Don't be impressed with the men in the long colorful robes who make a great show of being guardians of God's holy Book. Don't be impressed with the gold and silver donations from people with great wealth. But do be impressed with the old lady. She is surrounded by show-offs. But she is truly genuine. She expects no congratulations. She looks for no praise. She gets no approving glances from anyone. The blessing of God is on her, he said. Don't be carried away by outward show. The poor widow had nothing to make a show about. No one will ever hold her in high regard. Let me tell you, she has the ear of God. God listens to her.

Call to Faith
It is the thought that counts!
>We are called to be generous with our time.
>We are called to be generous with our talents.
>We are called to be generous with our energy.
>We are called to be generous with our words.
>But we are young.
>We don't have much money.
>We don't have much time.
>We don't have many talents.
>We aren't very polished with our words.

The widow woman didn't have much money, much time, or many talents, but she gave what she had with great heart. Jesus thought her action was magnificent.

>We are called to learn from her.

Call to Action
Some gestures of generosity must be expressed in the course of today's Mass—practical gestures to parents, to grandparents, to friends, to God. The children must be convinced that their seemingly small acts are magnified by God to merit great blessings.

Help the children plan and undertake a course of action at home or at school that would be supportive and helpful, in some small way, to the family or the school community.

Thirty-Third Sunday
in Ordinary Time

Gospel
A reading from the holy Gospel according to Mark (13:24–32)

Jesus said, "But in those days, after that suffering,
the sun will be darkened,
and the moon will not give its
light,
and the stars will be falling from heaven,
and the powers in the heavens
will be shaken.
Then they will see 'the Son of Man coming in clouds'
with great power and glory. Then he will send out the angels, and gather his elect from the four winds, from the
ends of the earth to the ends of heaven."

The gospel of the Lord.

Overview
Apocalyptic times. Dreadful scenario. The Christians for whom Mark is
writing are experiencing persecution, torture, and death. Will there be
no end to the bloodshed? No end to their pain?

God will not abandon God's people. Of that they can be assured.
Jesus will come in glory. We try to communicate a cosmic vision of God
to the children. Though the whole world passes away, God's love cannot pass away. God's love will encircle us for ever.

Children sometimes magnify their own troubles to apocalyptic pro-
portions. We can persuade them that there is hope in the gloomiest situation.

Exploring the Word of God
"You'll get awful news," Jesus said. "You'll hear stories of cities being
bombed, crops destroyed. There'll be hunger and famine. Every family
will be in mourning. There'll be no end to it. Death, destruction, bombs,
explosions, killing, murder, violence. Blood everywhere. Tears everywhere. Sadness everywhere. Land sucked under the sea. Volcanoes
erupting and black ash blotting out the light of the sun. The air pol-
luted, the earth contaminated, and water not fit to drink. Funerals

would go on day after day, hour after hour. Lines of coffins as far as the horizon. Streams of refugees fleeing from the terrors. Sickness, disease, death. No escape. Arrests, imprisonment, torture. The world gone mad."

But Jesus also said love would never die. Love would not fade way. Love would not be destroyed. Families would be held together by love. And love would get the better of fear. God's love would encircle the earth. God's love would be a light and a comfort to everyone. Everyone who believed would be safe with God.

Call to Faith

No matter how gloomy the situation, we are called to hope. God's love outlasts every disaster. We are called to be people of hope.

Call to Action

It might be a time to mention some social disasters like drugs or abortion.

It might be a time to mention unemployment or poverty.

It might be a time to mention sickness or disability.

We must have hope. We mustn't give up on ourselves or on each other.

Have someone recovering from a problem with alcoholism, drug abuse, or despair give a testimony to the children about the power of hope.

CHRIST THE KING

Gospel
A reading from the holy Gospel according to John (18:33–37)

Then Pilate entered the headquarters again, summoned Jesus, and asked him, "Are you the King of the Jews?" Jesus answered, "Do you ask this on your own, or did others tell you about me?" Pilate replied, "I am not a Jew, am I? Your own nation and the chief priests have handed you over to me. What have you done?" Jesus answered, "My kingdom is not from this world. If my kingdom were from this world my followers would be fighting to keep me from being handed over to the Jews. But as it is, my kingdom is not from here. Pilate asked him, "So you are a king?" Jesus answered, "You say that I am a king. For this I was born, and for this I came into the world, to testify to the truth. Everyone who belongs to the truth listens to my voice."

The gospel of the Lord.

Overview
Jesus the king. It's a title he rejected. He made it clear to Pilate that he had no ambitions to be king. The people tried to make him king but he ran from them. Yet in a beautiful compliment and for another purpose we have crowned him king. We call him the king of justice, the king of peace, the king of love. It's the kind of kingship that Jesus aspired to. He wants to lead us into a new kingdom where these virtues will have a preeminent place.

Jesus wants us to go with him and build a new world. He has the ideas. He looks to us for the muscle and the energy. He is calling us to follow him.

Focusing Experiences
We have to move quickly from the historical notion of king and kingship to a more poetic notion of king; from king of land and armies to king of ideas, king of the heart, king of the peace-lovers, king of the justice-seekers, king of the care-givers. It is among these last that the kingship of Jesus fits.

A song about justice could serve to introduce the homily.

Exploring the Word of God

Governor Pilate sat in the great chair of the council room surrounded by his officers and officials. Jesus was brought before him, having spent the night in the cells at the palace of the high priest Caiaphas. "Are you the king of the Jews?" Pilate asked Jesus. So the interview began. Pilate had good reason to ask this question. Did Jesus want to become king? Did Jesus want to overthrow Pilate? Did Jesus want to become king and put an an end to the rule of Governor Pilate? Did Jesus aspire to living in the palace? Was he the type who wanted to be surrounded by an army of servants and have his own elite palace guard? These were the accusations that had been made. Jesus' enemies said he wanted to be king. His enemies said he wanted to replace Pilate.

Jesus answered Pilate very simply. "I am not a king." Pilate made up his mind very quickly that Jesus was telling the truth. He could see that the man had no interest in becoming a king. And Pilate was astute at figuring these things. Jesus had no ambition to storm the palace or lead a revolt. Pilate could see that Jesus' eyes were not on earthly glory but on heaven, on the things of God. His talk was not about armies and palaces and soldiers and land, but about God. Jesus wanted people to change their ways. He wanted to convert them to God.

Pilate felt no threat from Jesus. He felt in no danger. But why was Jesus brought before him? Why did some people feel that he should be silenced? Who was afraid of the words of Jesus? It was obvious to Pilate that some kind of conspiracy against Jesus was afoot. But it had nothing to do with becoming a king of Jerusalem. Jesus certainly didn't want to become a king. There was no doubt about that.

Call to Faith

Jesus, you didn't want to become a king but yet you are our universal king.

You are our king of justice, because you want a world full of justice.

You are our king of goodness, because you want us to build a world where goodness will prevail.

You are our king of hope, because you want all of us to have hope of a new world.

You are our king of peace, because you want us all to live in peace.

You are our king of love, because you say that love and not hate must be at the center of what we say and do.

You are the king of our hearts to lead us in love, in peace, in justice, through our lives.

161

Call to Action

Make placards with captions reading "Justice," "Peace," "Love."

Other headlines might read, "Jesus, king of our hearts"; "King of Peace"; "King of Justice."

Sing songs of peace and justice and concern for our brothers and sisters.

Invite a two-minute testimony from someone who is working for justice.